C000280035

ALEXIS MICHALIK

Alexis Michalik is a French actor, au
French artist of Polish origin and a B

His original plays, which he has written and directed, include *Le Porteur d'histoire* (2011); *Le Cercle des illusionnistes* (2014); *Edmond* (2016); *Intra Muros* (2017) and *Une histoire d'amour* (2020). Both *Le Porteur* and *Le Cercle* were nominated at the 2014 Molière Awards, and Alexis won for Best Author and Best Director. All have received critical and commercial success, and are still running in Paris.

His adaptations include *Une folle journée*, based on *The Marriage of Figaro* by Beaumarchais (2005); *La Mégère à peu près apprivoisée*, based on *The Taming of the Shrew* (2006); *R&J*, based on *Romeo and Juliet* (2008); and *Carmen Rock & Soul Opéra* (2010).

Alexis has appeared in over fifty films, TV movies and series; directed two full-length feature films, based on his plays *Edmond* and *Une histoire d'amour*; and written a novel, *Loin*, which has sold over 100,000 copies.

WALEED AKHTAR

Waleed Akhtar is a writer and actor.

He was a Michael Grandage Company Futures bursary winner in 2021 and has been nominated for the Most Promising Playwright in the 2022 Evening Standard Theatre Awards. His work includes *The P Word* (Bush Theatre), *Kabul Goes Pop* (Brixton House/HighTide/ Colchester Mercury; UK tour), and a new commission from Audible as part of the Emerging Playwrights scheme. He created *Sholay on the Big Screen* supported by the Bush and co-created *I Don't Know What To Do* at the VAULT Festival 2020 (Evening Standard Pick of the Fest). His short film *Lost Paradise* was produced by UK Film Council, and he has contributed material for BBC Radio 4's *Sketchtopia* and *Newsjack*, and BBC3's *Famalam*.

As an actor his credits include *The Great* (Hulu), *Cruella* (Disney), *Salmon Fishing in the Yemen* (Kudos), and he has worked with theatres including The Young Vic, Brimingham Rep, Bush and Chichester Festival Theatre.

Alexis Michalik

THE ART OF ILLUSION

Le Cercle des illusionnistes

Translated by
Waleed Akhtar

NICK HERN BOOKS
London
www.nickhernbooks.co.uk

A Nick Hern Book

The Art of Illusion first published in Great Britain in 2022 as a paperback original by Nick Hern Books Limited, The Glasshouse, 49a Goldhawk Road, London W12 8QP, by arrangement with Editions Albin Michel

Cover image: n9design.com

Designed and typeset by Nick Hern Books, London
Printed in Great Britain by Mimeo Ltd, Huntingdon, Cambridgeshire PE29 6XX

A CIP catalogue record for this book is available from the British Library

ISBN 978 1 83904 148 8

Le Cercle des illusionnistes was first performed at Théâtre de La Pépinière-Opéra, Paris, on 22 January 2014, directed by Alexis Michalik, and with a cast including Jeanne Arènes, Maud Baecker, Michel Derville, Arnaud Dupont, Vincent Joncquez and Mathieu Métral.

The play received its English premiere, as *The Art of Illusion*, at Hampstead Theatre Downstairs, London, on 17 December 2022. The cast was as follows:

CATHERINE	Rina Fatania
APRIL	Bettrys Jones
THE WATCHMAKER	Martin Hyder
GEORGES	Norah Lopez Holden
DECEMBER	Brian Martin
JEAN	Kwaku Mills

All other parts played by the company

Director	Tom Jackson Greaves
Designer	Simon Kenny
Lighting	Matt Haskins
Sound	Yvonne Gilbert
Illusion Consultant	Ben Hart

6

Characters

THE WATCHMAKER
APRIL
DECEMBER
THE CAFÉ OWNER
LOUIS
CATHERINE
GEORGES
JEAN
THE BOOKSELLER
ANTONIA
THE MAN FROM THE AUDIENCE
GERARD
LOUISE
MARGOT
MANUEL
SUZANNE
WILLIAM
THE CUSTOMER
MARIUS
TROUILLET
MADAME GABRIELLE
LALLEMENT
LUCIEN
CHARLES
MADEMOISELLE JOSIANE
THE NIGHT WATCHMAN
JEANNE

Words in square brackets are unspoken.

This text went to press before the end of rehearsals and so may differ slightly from the play as performed.

1. Prologue

The Mechanical Turk

THE WATCHMAKER (*speaking to the audience*). A red scarf
  is waved in front of your eyes.
  Then tucked into a hand. The hand opens.
  Empty.
  Where has the scarf gone? Your brain cells start whirring:
  Some people know, some keep looking, others don't want
  to know.
  It's all a matter of perception.
  Like how the hands of time are turning at the same speed for
  everyone,
  Yet a child waits an eternity for summer, while an old man
  watches a year pass in the blink of an eye.
  Right now the Earth on which we stand is turning on its axis;
  but it's also turning around the Sun. While the Solar System
  is turning around our Galaxy, and our Galaxy is turning too.
  So we can all agree that everything is turning? Right? Yet we
  cannot see it.
  If we accept that we are constantly turning, why can't we
  accept the scarf has disappeared?

1776: The Russian Imperial Court, an inventor presents an
automaton. It's a male bust, in the form of a not-very-PC
Turk, complete with turban and tash (what? It was 1776); it
stood on a cabinet, about a metre wide, which contained the
mechanism. In front of the Turk, was an ivory chessboard.
This was a chess-playing automaton that systematically won
all its games.

1805: The French city of Blois, Jean-Eugène Robert was
born, son of a watchmaker, grandson of a watchmaker.

1861: The Parisian suburb of Montreuil, Catherine
Schuering, daughter of a shoemaker, married to a bootmaker,
gave birth to young Georges.

1954: The Parisian suburb of Aubervilliers, December was born and abandoned at birth. A Catholic orphanage took him in. To make sure he would never abandon a child himself, December decided that he would never have a child. At twenty he got the snip (a vasectomy).

1984, 16th June, it was a regular day at the office for December. After having tried his hand unsuccessfully at several trades, his main occupation now was 'lifting' wallets in the Paris Métro.

On this occasion he 'lifts' a bag. In the bag is a passport. He opens it. He can't help but notice how beautiful the woman in the photo is.

2. 19 June 1984, 8.32 p.m., Paris

France vs. Yugoslavia

A Parisian bistro.
The third group match in the UEFA European Football Championship is on TV: France vs. Yugoslavia.

TELEVISION COMMENTARY (*voice-over*). France versus Yugoslavia.
France are already into the semis of this European Championship, after winning their opening two games, and the host nation could be well on their way to making history with their first major trophy. No such luck for Yugoslavia, having already lost both their games, they are definitely going home empty-handed.

DECEMBER. April?

APRIL. December?

DECEMBER. April?

APRIL. Yes, that's me.

DECEMBER. You're smaller than I thought.

APRIL. Really?

DECEMBER. No, no, I mean…
   (*Holding the bag out to her.*)

APRIL. Thank you.
   (*She grabs the bag and rummages through it.*)
   I'm not particularly hopeful.

DECEMBER. Best way to be…

APRIL (*her face lighting up*). Wow! Everything's there!

DECEMBER. Right then.

APRIL. Thank you.

DECEMBER. It's nothing.

APRIL. You found it in the Métro?

DECEMBER. Yeah.

APRIL. Where exactly?

DECEMBER. …On the… platform.

APRIL. Actually, of course, the money's missing.

DECEMBER. …Er, well, have a good evening.

APRIL. Wait. I need to say thanks. Can I get you a drink?
   (*Trying to be funny.*)
   Unless I'm too small.

DECEMBER. No, no, you're a very good size, sorry I mean…

APRIL. You probably have things to do.

DECEMBER. Umm not [really]…

APRIL. The football! When will I ever meet a man that isn't obsessed with the football?

DECEMBER. I'm not. I barely know that it's France vee Yugoslavia.

APRIL. Really? It's a big match.

DECEMBER. But we've already qualified. Or so I hear. I don't know.

THE CAFÉ OWNER. What'll you have, ladies and gents?

APRIL (*looking at* DECEMBER). Are we having a drink?

DECEMBER. Er… Why not?

THE CAFÉ OWNER. What'll it be?

DECEMBER (*sitting down*). A pint.

THE CAFÉ OWNER. One pint of lager and – ?

APRIL. A lemonade for me please.

THE CAFÉ OWNER. Oh congrats… boy or a girl?

APRIL. I beg your pardon?

THE CAFÉ OWNER. 'A lemonade', and you've got that glow,
I can always tell when someone's pregnant.
(*Off* APRIL.) Does Daddy not know… I should learn to keep
my mouth shut.

DECEMBER. Er…

APRIL. No, no, no!
(*To* DECEMBER.) It's just, I have a friend who's pregnant
and out of solidarity, I promised that…

DECEMBER. I'll just have a Coke.

APRIL. You don't have to.

DECEMBER. I'd love a Coke.

THE CAFÉ OWNER (*moving away*). One Coke and one
lemonade.
(*Leaves the stage*.) And definitely no buns in the oven.

DECEMBER. Well, that was more embarrassing than normal.

APRIL. A man and woman can have a non-alcoholic drink
together, without all the assumptions.

DECEMBER. Yes…

APRIL. It's the eighties!

DECEMBER. Can't actually remember my last drink with
a woman.

APRIL. Really?

DECEMBER.... A long time.

Brief silence.

APRIL. So, December.

DECEMBER. Yeah...

APRIL (*turning towards him*). April.

DECEMBER. Yeah, I know.

APRIL. December, April.

DECEMBER. Yeah.

APRIL. It's crazy, the probability of...

DECEMBER. Of?

APRIL. Sorry, it's irrelevant.

DECEMBER. What?

APRIL. I like mathematics. Figures. Logic.
  Do you have any children?

DECEMBER. What?

APRIL. That came out wrong. Sorry!

DECEMBER. No. I don't have any children.

APRIL. Right.

DECEMBER. In fact, at twenty I decided to...

APRIL. Yes?

DECEMBER. Nothing. And you? What about you?

APRIL. Me?

DECEMBER. You?

APRIL. What?

DECEMBER. Children?

APRIL. No. Not yet.

Brief silence.

DECEMBER. So, maths?

APRIL. Do you believe in God? The cross around your neck.

DECEMBER (*touching the cross with his hand*). No, I was brought up by the...

APRIL. The?

DECEMBER....Do you believe in God?

APRIL. Me, I'm a Fundamental Cartesian.

DECEMBER. A what?

APRIL. Rationalist.

DECEMBER. Er...

APRIL. Atheist.

DECEMBER. Right. Know that one.

APRIL. But nowadays I believe that something exists. I don't know what but something. Chance. Fate. Magic.

DECEMBER (*sceptical*). Magic?

APRIL. You don't agree?

DECEMBER *pouts eloquently.*

THE CAFÉ OWNER (*placing the drinks on the table*). One Coke and one lemonade.

APRIL (*to* THE CAFÉ OWNER). Are you good at adding up?

THE CAFÉ OWNER. It's part of the job.

APRIL. Alright. Work this out, in your heads. Both of you.

DECEMBER. I'm not very good.

APRIL. I'll go slowly.
One thousand. Plus forty. Plus a thousand. Plus thirty.

DECEMBER. Wait, wait.

THE CAFÉ OWNER. That's easy.

DECEMBER (*glaring at* THE CAFÉ OWNER)....Okay.

APRIL. Plus a thousand. Plus twenty. Plus a thousand. Plus ten. Equals?

THE CAFÉ OWNER. Five thousand.

DECEMBER. Five thousand.

APRIL. Four thousand, one hundred.
Four thousand and ninety plus ten equals four thousand, one hundred.

THE CAFÉ OWNER (*who's just recounted*). I was sure it made five thousand.
(*Goes away, puzzled.*)

DECEMBER. What was that all about?

APRIL. Magic.

3. 14 June 1871, Paris

Georges

LOUIS. Catherine? Catherine?

CATHERINE. I'm in the bedroom. No need to shout.

A middle-class apartment in Paris.
A ten-year-old boy, GEORGES.
His father, LOUIS. *His mother,* CATHERINE.

LOUIS (*entering*). Have you seen Georges' boots?

CATHERINE. Behind the armchair?

LOUIS. They're not there! I've already looked!

CATHERINE. Louis, who are we visiting this time?

LOUIS. A client who's just patented a type of 'incandescent light bulb'. I don't know what that is either.
(*Calling out loud.*) Georges, where are your boots?

GEORGES (*entering*). Papa, please, I want to wear my shoes!

LOUIS. I told you to wear your boots. So you'll put your boots on.

GEORGES. Boots, boots, always boots…

CATHERINE (*to* LOUIS). Look under the bed.

LOUIS (*finding the boots under the bed*). Here they are.
(*Holding the boots out to* GEORGES.) Boots are the instruments that enable a man to stand up straight and walk forward, Georges. They must be treated accordingly.

GEORGES (*lowering his face*). I prefer my shoes.

LOUIS *and* CATHERINE *exchange silent looks*.

CATHERINE. Georges, I need you to listen to a story.
The Queen of Holland used to dance a lot. A ball every two weeks.
But whenever she danced her feet ached enormously.
She called for a new bootmaker. The best in the land!
Henricus Schuering, a young man of modest origin, was brought to her.
He made such wonderful boots that the Queen decreed he would marry her chambermaid.
Theirs was an extremely happy marriage and they had three children.

LOUIS. The eldest was called Catherine.

GEORGES. Catherine? Like Mama?

CATHERINE. What a clever boy you are.
Our family business was destroyed by fire.
With the business ruined, Henricus, my father, went into exile. We all settled in Paris and he arranged for my sisters and I to work in a factory.

LOUIS. A boot factory.

GEORGES. And you two met in this boot factory?

CATHERINE. Exactly. Your papa was an apprentice bootmaker.

LOUIS. Georges, ever since your mother and I got married,
ever since we decided to start our own business, not a day in
our life has gone by that hasn't been devoted to boots.

CATHERINE.... Put your boots on, Georges.

GEORGES *puts his boots on.*

4. 14 June 1871, Blois

The Priory

THE WATCHMAKER. Are you here for the reception?

LOUIS. No, we're collecting for charity.
Of course we're here for the reception.

*They join the reception. There's a crowd of people, shouts,
laughter, champagne.*

CATHERINE. As we speak, millions of feet are walking all
over the planet, Georges. Some more delicate than others.
We are here to provide them all with footwear.

LOUIS. Today, we have seventy-five employees working for us
in our building on Boulevard Saint-Martin.
And one day, that factory will be yours.

5. 19 June 1984, 9.02 p.m., Paris

Goal

DECEMBER *stands up to watch the match*.

THE TV (*voice-over*). And Sestic scores... Goal for Yugoslavia!

DECEMBER. Bloody hell!

THE TV (*voice-over*). Sestic opens the scoring in the thirty-second minute!

DECEMBER. Oh shit!

THE TV (*voice-over*). France will be disappointed, these Yugoslavians aren't giving anything away...

DECEMBER. Shiiiit. We'll come back... (*He realises that* APRIL *is silently watching him.*) to the point that the TV is so loud. No?

APRIL. Really.

DECEMBER.... So what do you do for a living?

APRIL. I'm a designer.

DECEMBER.... an interior designer?

APRIL. No, I specialise in engineering.

DECEMBER. Of what?

APRIL. I build safes.
Safe-deposit boxes.
Bank vaults.

DECEMBER (*impressed*). Really?

APRIL. And you?

DECEMBER. Me?

APRIL. To earn a living?

DECEMBER. Er... this and that.

APRIL. Have you got any qualifications?

DECEMBER. A Vocational Training Certificate in Mechanics.

APRIL. A Vocational Training Certificate in Mechanics.

DECEMBER.... Anything mechanical.

APRIL. Okay.

DECEMBER. Motorbikes, cars, mopeds, electricity.

APRIL. Okay.

DECEMBER. That's it. But I have other interests.

APRIL. Like what?

DECEMBER. Films. Old films mainly.

APRIL. But you like football better?

DECEMBER. I already told you, I'm not like other guys you know, not big on football.

APRIL. Not the impression I get. Did your dad ever take you to see football matches?

DECEMBER. Errm... I never knew my dad.

APRIL. Sorry.

DECEMBER. Or my mum.

APRIL. Oh shit.

DECEMBER. Actually I grew up in an orphanage.

APRIL. Ah, right.

DECEMBER. A Catholic one.

APRIL. Oh dear.

DECEMBER. Hence the cross.

APRIL. Okay.

DECEMBER. But otherwise, everything's fine.

There's a hushed silence.

APRIL. So what else do you like?

DECEMBER. Well... when I was a kid, I had a thing about magic.

APRIL. No, really?

DECEMBER. Yes. I had a book by Robert-Houdin, an old magic book that I knew by heart. I must have read it a hundred times.

APRIL. By who?

DECEMBER. Robert-Houdin.

APRIL. You mean Houdini?

DECEMBER. No, no, no. Everyone gets them mixed up. Houdini was an American who used that name in tribute to Robert-Houdin. Robert-Houdin was a Frenchman. A genius. Before he came along, magic meant guys with pointy hats and tumblers, street performers. He put on an evening suit and took magic to the theatre.

APRIL. A magician.

DECEMBER. A magician, watchmaker, mechanic, inventor...

APRIL. What did he invent?

DECEMBER. Loads of things. An alarm-clock lighter, a mystery clock and not just clocks, at the end of his life, a light bulb.

APRIL. A light bulb?

DECEMBER. Yes, a light bulb. An incandescent light bulb.

6. 14 June 1871, Blois

An Incandescent Light Bulb

Dazzling light.
A demonstration of electricity: incandescent light bulbs
illuminate the stage.
Murmurs of admiration. Applause.

LOUIS. That light is amazing!

CATHERINE. It's magic!

LOUIS. We must get the same for the shop!

CATHERINE. What do you think, Georges?
   (*She cannot find him.*)
   Georges? Georges?

LOUIS. Don't worry. He must be in the garden.

7. The Watchmaker

GEORGES *isn't in the garden; he's upstairs in a study.*
THE WATCHMAKER *is sitting in the shadows. He is sixty-five*
years old.

THE WATCHMAKER. Some believe that life is a straight line.
   But life is a circle, since we're all turning.
   It's an eternal recommencement.
   Knowing when it will be your turn is the only question.
   (*Without turning around.*)
   Come in, Georges. Come closer.

GEORGES. How do you know my name?

THE WATCHMAKER. I know a lot of things.

   GEORGES *approaches him.*

   I know how to make a coin appear, or disappear.
   (*He performs a little magic trick.*)

How to make a child fly through the air,
How to create light.
And I know that the future your parents have planned for
you does not exactly delight you.

GEORGES. How do you know that?

THE WATCHMAKER. I remember a little boy whose father
wanted him to become a watchmaker. His own father had
been a watchmaker; his grandfather had been a watchmaker.
But little Jean liked automatons.

GEORGES. Automatons?

8. 19 June 1984, 9.15 p.m., Paris

Automatons

APRIL. Automatons?

DECEMBER. Yes, automatons. They're a kind of robot, or at
least the ancestors of robots. Like the Mechanical Turk, or
the Digesting Duck...

APRIL. The what?

DECEMBER. Vaucanson's Digesting Duck. It was a duck.

APRIL. I got that bit.

DECEMBER. Not a real duck. But it could waddle, move its
head, quack. It could even drink water, eat grain and most
important of all shit...

APRIL....most impressive.

DECEMBER. It was, the guy invented a mechanical digestive
process!

APRIL. And the other one, the...

DECEMBER....Mechanical Turk?

APRIL. Yes.

DECEMBER. It was the bust of a Turk who played chess.

APRIL. A Turk?

DECEMBER. Yeah, a Turk. Complete with moustache, sabre, and turban.

APRIL.... who played chess.

DECEMBER. He won every game.

APRIL. How long ago was that?

DECEMBER. Eighteenth century.

APRIL. Now that is impressive!

DECEMBER. Yeah.
But Robert-Houdin's automatons were even more impressive.

9. 1825–1871, Blois

Jean

THE WATCHMAKER. Fate comes in several forms.

1825, in a bookshop in Blois. JEAN *is then twenty years old.*

JEAN (*entering the bookshop*). Good evening!

THE BOOKSELLER. I'll be with you in a minute!

THE WATCHMAKER. Believers call it God, sceptics call it coincidence, the Arabs call it *mektoub*.

JEAN. I've come to collect my handbook on watchmaking.

THE BOOKSELLER. Yes, I'm coming!

THE WATCHMAKER. For Jean, fate first came in the form of a bookseller.

THE BOOKSELLER (*handing him a book*). Here you are! Pay
me tomorrow.

THE WATCHMAKER. Perhaps she was tired, or in a hurry.

JEAN. How much do I owe you?

THE BOOKSELLER. Tomorrow, tomorrow!

THE WATCHMAKER. Only when he got home did Jean realise
there had been a mistake: the book he held in his hands was
Conjuring and Card Tricks.
It was too late to return it.
So he read a page. Then another. Then the rest of the book.

GEORGES. A book on magic?

THE WATCHMAKER (*handing the book to* GEORGES).
Exactly.
The following day, Jean began practising.
In less than a month, he could make coins, balls and scarves
disappear.

JEAN *makes a scarf disappear.*

10. 19 June 1984, 9.20 p.m., Paris

Sleight of Hand

DECEMBER. Okay. You see this bottle?
(*Points to the newspaper in* APRIL*'s handbag.*)
Do you mind?
(*Takes newspaper.*)
I place the paper over the bottle. Take hold of the bottle.
(*Bottle disappears.*)

APRIL. Where is it?

DECEMBER. Magic.

APRIL. Where'd you put it?

DECEMBER *points to her handbag, she takes out the bottle.*

No!

DECEMBER. Do you want me to explain?

APRIL. No, no, no, don't.

DECEMBER (*gives back the crumpled paper*). Sorry.

APRIL. That was brilliant.

DECEMBER. It was easy

APRIL. So you're a magician?

DECEMBER. Just for fun.

APRIL. What else can you do? Can you make a dove appear?

DECEMBER. That's way too old-fashioned.

He does the 'napkin into paper flower' trick and gives it to APRIL.

APRIL. I love it!

DECEMBER *lights a cigarette.*

DECEMBER. D'you want a cigarette?

APRIL. I don't smoke.

DECEMBER. Oh, right… So how many months pregnant are you then?

APRIL. Three. How did you know?

DECEMBER. I didn't. I was joking from before.

APRIL (*her secret now out*). Oh shit.

DECEMBER. Well, your husband must be pleased?

APRIL. I don't have a husband.

DECEMBER (*hopeful*). Ah.

APRIL.…Fiancé.

DECEMBER (*disappointed*). Ah… So maths.

11. 23 July 1828, Tours

Stew

THE WATCHMAKER. The second time that fate stepped into Jean's life came in the form of a bowl of stew.
On the 23rd July 1828, Jean returned home from a village fête feeling ravenous. Now twenty-three, he was living and working at a watchmaker's in Tours.

JEAN (*calling out loud*). Marie! I'm finishing off the stew!

THE WATCHMAKER. He had no inkling of the extraordinary consequences eating this stew would have on the rest of his existence.
Had he gone to bed hungry, he probably would have spent his entire life working as a small-town watchmaker.
But instead he wolfed it down.
The bottom of the saucepan was coated in verdigris. Do you know what verdigris is, Georges?

GEORGES. A poison produced from copper sulphate.

THE WATCHMAKER. Clever boy!
Now Jean fell seriously ill. Hovering between life and death.
In his delirious state, he decided to go back home to his parents.
Feverish and exhausted, he pulled himself out of bed and left the house.
He took the stagecoach that ran between Tours and Blois.
On the way, he leant out of the window to get some fresh air.
At that moment the coach lurched over a rock, the door opened and Jean fell out onto the road.
The coach continued on its way...

GEORGES (*after a while*). Did he die?

THE WATCHMAKER. Nearly.
He remained unconscious for several hours, didn't even realise that he was being carried by unknown arms into a strange bedroom.
When he woke up, he thought he could hear an Italian tenor singing in time with the sound of a horse's hoof...

12. 1828–1871, Blois

The Conjuror

In the caravan, THE WATCHMAKER *becomes* THE CONJUROR.

THE CONJUROR. Si è svegliato! Miracolo! Santa Vergine! Antonia! E sveglio!
[*He's woken up! What a miracle! Holy Virgin Mary, he's woken up! Antonia!*]

The horses whinny, the caravan comes to a halt.

ANTONIA. E sveglio?
[*He's awake, is he?*]

THE CONJUROR. Perché hai fermato la carrozza, siamo già in ritardo!
[*Why have you stopped? We're already late!*]

ANTONIA. Ma se è stato lei a dirmi di…
[*But you were the one who told me to…*]

THE CONJUROR. Sono io che ti ho detto cosa?
[*I was the one who told you to?*]

ANTONIA. Si!
[*Yes!*]

THE CONJUROR. Sono io che ti ho detto cosa?
[*I was the one who told you to?*]

ANTONIA. Si! [*Yes!*]

THE CONJUROR. Muoviti, presto, non arriveremo mai prima di stasera!
[*Get going, get going, we'll never arrive in time tonight!*]

The caravan starts moving again. THE CONJUROR *turns to* JEAN *and speaks with an Italian accent.*

Forgive her. Antonia was sure you were going to die, even though I assured her otherwise.

JEAN (*very weak*). You're Italian?

THE CONJUROR (*with an Italian accent*). Don't speak, don't get up, don't move, every bone in your body is broken.

JEAN *remains motionless for a moment.*

I was joking. You're fine. I'll help you.

THE CONJUROR *bends over* JEAN *to help him get up.*

ANTONIA. Stiamo per arrivare ad Angers!
[*We're coming into Angers!*]

JEAN. Angers?

THE CONJUROR. Yes, Angers. We're performing a show here. Cough.

JEAN *coughs and grimaces with pain.*

Hurts? Must have cracked a rib, possibly two. But your limbs are alright. There's nothing broken.

JEAN. Are you a doctor?

THE CONJUROR. Yes, luckily for you I was a doctor, in another life.

13. 24 July 1828, Angers

The Little Travelling Theatre

THE CONJUROR. Avanti, Antonia, avanti!
[*Move on, Antonia, move on!*]

They're in a public square in Angers. ANTONIA *moves the horses forward.* THE CONJUROR *watches what she's doing, while* JEAN *observes everything, leaning on a walking stick.*

(*To* JEAN.) It's a very simple mechanical process: the caravan is on a kind of rail, which enables it to double in length whenever we stop, converting it into a little travelling theatre.

JEAN. Are you a magician?

THE CONJUROR. Absolutely. I was a doctor, then I became
a conjuror.
(*To the public at large*.) Step right up, ladies and gentlemen,
step right up! The Great Torrini is in town!

14. The Show

THE CONJUROR *is halfway through his performance in the*
caravan.
A number of spectators are watching his tricks.
ANTONIA *is applauding.*

ANTONIA. Bravissimo!

THE CONJUROR. Grazie mille!
But these tricks, ladies and gentlemen, are just the warm-up.
Now, sir, I'm going to ask you to blindfold me.

ANTONIA (*holding out the blindfold so people can feel it*).
Toccate, toccate.

THE CONJUROR. Go ahead, make sure I can't see through the
blindfold.

THE MAN FROM THE AUDIENCE. That should do it.

THE CONJUROR. The gentleman has put a blindfold on me,
now here is a pack of cards. Would you check that this pack
is quite normal, sir.

THE MAN FROM THE AUDIENCE. Indeed it is.

THE CONJUROR. Shuffle the pack, please. Do you know how
to play Piquet?

THE MAN FROM THE AUDIENCE. I play regularly.

THE CONJUROR. Perfect. Allow me to deal the cards while
I tell you what's going to happen: I'm going to announce
which cards will be in your hand, and I'm going to beat you,
without removing my blindfold.

The audience laughs.

15. The Takings

ANTONIA. Cento cinquanta, cento sessanta, cento settanta, centosettantuno! [*150... 160... 170... 171!*]

THE CONJUROR. One hundred and seventy-one. Not bad for a premiere. Tomorrow, there'll be twice as many in the audience. Did you enjoy the show?

JEAN. Very much. You're so skilful.

THE CONJUROR. Did you understand how some of the tricks work?

JEAN. Some of them.

THE CONJUROR. But not the card trick with the blindfold?

JEAN. That one was very clever.

THE CONJUROR. It's my favourite.

JEAN. If I understood it correctly, just before you deal the cards, you replace the pack that's been shuffled with another specially prepared pack... helped by a little device probably hidden up your sleeve like... this one?

JEAN *removes a little box from his pocket and hands it to the astonished* CONJUROR. ANTONIA *and* THE CONJUROR *exchange looks. They hadn't expected this.*

THE CONJUROR. This little device was given to me by our dear friend – and trickster – on his deathbed. I have put it to a less lucrative and less dangerous use. How did you work it out?

JEAN (*examining the device*). When you raised your voice, I heard a little squeak. The mechanism's worn out. Needs replacing. It'll take a couple of days, three at the most.

THE CONJUROR. Are you a mechanic?

JEAN. A watchmaker – (*Handing him back the device*.) and a conjuror's apprentice.

THE CONJUROR. The apprentice is already showing promise.

JEAN. Would you mind if I came on the road with you?

ANTONIA. Incredibile.

Ne sa una più del diavolo.

[*Incredible. This little devil has more than one trick up his sleeve.*]

16. 3 August 1828, On the Road to Angoulême

A Storm is Brewing

The storm is rumbling.
In the caravan, THE CONJUROR *is teaching* JEAN *a few tricks.*

THE CONJUROR. Whenever you ask someone to choose a card, shuffle the cards without making a show of it.

JEAN. Like this?

JEAN *lets the pack of cards cascade down from one hand to the other.*

THE CONJUROR. No, nothing fancy. Never fancy. Just do the trick. Keep things simple, you'll earn the volunteer's trust; you'll flatter their intelligence and they'll be much less likely not to see anything coming.

The caravan starts rocking dangerously from side to side.

Antonia, stai bene?

ANTONIA. Ma porca di quella miseria!

The rain suddenly starts pouring down. There's a peal of thunder. The horses whinny and bolt up a slope.

JEAN. What's happening?

THE CONJUROR. What was meant to happen. The horses are bolting.
(*In Italian.*) Frena, Antonia, frena!

ANTONIA. Non posso!

THE CONJUROR. Grab hold of something and say a prayer.

JEAN. Our Father which art in Heaven…

The brakes on the caravan fail.

HELP!

The caravan crashes down a slope.

THE CONJUROR. Jump, Antonia!

JEAN. Don't tell her to jump!

THE CONJUROR (*to* JEAN). Hold on tight!

The caravan topples over and crashes to the ground.
The passengers are thrown out. Semi-darkness. Rain lashing
down. Lightning.

ANTONIA (*barely visible*). Edmond! Edmond!

JEAN. Antonia, are you alright?

ANTONIA. Si!

JEAN. Are you hurt?

ANTONIA. Sto bene, sto bene, ma dov'é il Conte?
[*I'm okay, I'm okay, but where's the Count?*]

JEAN. Who?

ANTONIA (*with a strong Italian accent*). Torrini! Where is he?

JEAN. I don't know.

A peal of thunder, very close by.

ANTONIA. Edmond!

Thunder and lightning flood the stage.

17.

The Great Prompter

THE CONJUROR *is lying in the caravan.*
It's still dark, but the light has changed: there's a rather strange candlelit atmosphere. JEAN *gazes around him, open-mouthed.*

THE CONJUROR. I'm done for. In this life, I'm done for.
(*Trying to get up.*)
Broken leg, fractured bone, dislocated shoulder. A magician can't perform without shoulders in working order.
(*Suddenly very serious.*)
If I can't perform tomorrow. I'll kill myself.

JEAN. What did you say?

THE CONJUROR (*speaking without an accent*). I'll kill myself, I'm telling you.
I've had so many lives, young Jean.
I've had so many names.

JEAN. Your accent.

THE CONJUROR. Your turn will come.

JEAN. You've lost your accent.

THE CONJUROR. Your turn will come, Jean-Eugène Robert.

JEAN. How do you know my full name?

The storm roars even louder.

THE CONJUROR (*getting up*). I know a lot of things.
I've had so many lives.

JEAN. Don't get up!

THE CONJUROR. I introduced Euripides to his Electra; I was the one who presented young William to Queen Elizabeth...

JEAN. I must be dreaming.

THE CONJUROR. I am a dream, an illusion, the Great Prompter, the spirit of entertainers.

ANTONIA (*off*). Signor Gianni!

JEAN. I must be dreaming.

Thunder rumbles.

THE CONJUROR. And tomorrow I'll kill myself with a bullet to the head.

ANTONIA. SIGNOR GIANNI! SIGNOR GIANNI!

There's a huge crack of thunder. THE CONJUROR *vanishes.*

JEAN. Antonia!

ANTONIA (*entering*). Where's Torrini?

JEAN (*pointing to* THE CONJUROR). There!

ANTONIA. He's not in the caravan!
Oh my God, if he's hurt himself, he won't be able to perform, and if he can't perform... (*Noticing the window.*) La finestra! He's gone through the window! SIGNOR TORRINI!

ANTONIA *leaps outside.* JEAN *looks at the the window that's been pushed out.*

JEAN (*shaking himself out of his reverie*). Antonia, be careful! He's got a broken leg and a dislocated shoulder!

ANTONIA. SIGNOR TORRINI!

THE CONJUROR (*offstage in a plaintive voice*). Antonia...

ANTONIA. Non potrà esibirsi! Non potrà esibirsi!
[*He won't be able to perform!*]

JEAN....I'll take his place!

ANTONIA (*coming back*). Pardon?

JEAN. The show in Angoulême. I'll take his place.

ANTONIA. Va bene!

Lightning. Peal of thunder.

18. 4 August 1828, Angoulême – 14 June 1871, Blois

Premiere

ANTONIA (*to the public at large*). Ladies and gentlemen! Step right up, step right up! Today the Great... Torrini is performing in your magnificent town of Angers for the very first time! This afternoon!

JEAN *is feeling nervous as he gets ready.*
Leaning on a crutch, THE CONJUROR *watches him from afar, a smile on his face. He then turns back into* THE WATCHMAKER.

THE WATCHMAKER (*to* GEORGES). A debut performance is a show an artiste remembers all his life.

ANTONIA. Step right up, step right up, don't be shy!

THE WATCHMAKER. Anxiety gets you in its grip, words stick in your throat, legs shake. Then the curtain opens and the audience is there.
A state that exists nowhere else except on stage.
A mix of ecstasy and terror, an *obscure clarity*.

GEORGES. Were you afraid?

THE WATCHMAKER. Who said I was talking about myself?

GEORGES *smiles*.

What a clever boy he is, this Georges.

LOUIS. Georges!

THE WATCHMAKER (*to* GEORGES). Your turn will come. You'll do great things.

LOUIS. Georges! Georges! Where were you? We've been looking for you everywhere!

GEORGES. I was with the gentleman!

LOUIS. Which gentleman, Georges? There's no one here but you.

GEORGES (*realising he's alone*). But... I...

LOUIS. This boy has far too much imagination.

CATHERINE (*putting her arm around* GEORGES' *shoulder*).
Come on, Georges, it's already very late.

GEORGES *looks around him.*
He finds a book, the book THE WATCHMAKER *gave him.*
He picks it up and follows his parents.

19. 19 June 1984, 9.29 p.m., Paris

Café

DECEMBER *is sitting on his own in the café watching the TV.*

THE TV (*voice-over*). Still one–nil to Yugoslavia.
It's by no means the best match the French squad have
played...

APRIL *returns to the table.*

DECEMBER. I should be off. Thanks for the drink.

APRIL (*watching the match*). We're losing.

DECEMBER. Yes. One–nil. That's life.

APRIL. You can't leave without finishing your story. So he
became a magician?

DECEMBER. Robert-Houdin? Not then.

APRIL. Why not?

DECEMBER. He got married and had children.
His wife didn't really encourage him to stay on the road.

APRIL. So it was his wife's fault!

DECEMBER. No, yes, partly?

APRIL. What did he become?

DECEMBER. A watchmaker. Like his father.

APRIL. So when did he become a magician, then?

DECEMBER. Er… I don't remember. Years later.
  Well, goodbye then.

APRIL. You can tell me the rest next time.

DECEMBER (*about to leave*). Sure.

APRIL (*holding him back*). Thanks again for the bag.
  If it wasn't for fate, you wouldn't have found it, and I wouldn't
  have heard the story of Robert-Houdin.

DECEMBER. I suppose.

He's on the point of leaving, then comes back.
He places a watch on the table, APRIL's watch, which he's
just stolen from her.
She doesn't understand.

APRIL. That's my watch!

DECEMBER. I didn't find your bag. I stole it. That's what I do.
  I steal bags. There's no fate. There's no magic. Just a trick.

APRIL. There was a present in my bag.

DECEMBER. I know.

APRIL *rummages through the bag that* DECEMBER *has*
given back.

APRIL. Didn't you open it?

DECEMBER. No.

She takes out a gift-wrapped present, the size of a book.

APRIL (*holding it out to him*). Open it. It's for you.

DECEMBER. Listen, I'm sorry about all this…

APRIL (*softly*). Open it.

He opens the present.
It's a book: An Artiste's Life *by Jean-Eugène Robert-Houdin.*
DECEMBER *is completely taken aback.*

DECEMBER (*in a very low voice*).…Is this a joke?

APRIL. No.

DECEMBER. This is my book. The one I read when I was little.

APRIL. What were you saying about fate?
(*Pointing to the TV.*)
I think we've just equalised.

DECEMBER *can't take his eyes off the book.*

20. 20 June 1984, Paris

Métro

DECEMBER *and* GERARD, *his best friend, are in the Métro.*

GERARD. Stop reading that book.

DECEMBER (*his nose in the book*). Gerard, it's bloody crazy.
The woman is crazy. This is crazy.

GERARD (*stealing his neighbour's wallet*). No, no, no. What's
crazy was the match. Into the semis! Back from two–nil
down, crazy! Actually, what woman are you talking about?

DECEMBER. She's not just beautiful, she's brilliant, too!

GERARD (*counting the money in the wallet under*
DECEMBER). One hundred, two hundred, three hundred
francs. Who?

DECEMBER. The woman in the Métro. The woman with the
bag. April!

GERARD (*stopping*). Again, what are you talking about?

DECEMBER. The woman with the passport in her bag. I called
her. Gave her back her bag.

GERARD. You did what?

DECEMBER. Gave her bag back.

GERARD. Are you out of your mind? Didn't she report you?

DECEMBER. How did she know about Robert-Houdin?

GERARD *stares at* DECEMBER.

GERARD. What the hell are you talking about?

21. 20 June 1984, Paris

Office

LOUISE. Wait a minute! Let me make sure I heard you right: you followed this man, this random man into the Métro and dropped your bag in front of him on purpose?

APRIL (*triumphant*). And he brought me back my bag!

LOUISE. Yes, babe, but without the money.

APRIL. And without opening the present!

LOUISE. You tellin' me you refused to go to the cinema with me for the Renoir retrospective, so this man, this September...

APRIL. December.

LOUISE. Whatever! So this good-for-nothing petty criminal could talk to you about chess-playing robots?

APRIL. Automatons.

LOUISE. Same difference. You told him you're engaged, right?

APRIL. Louise, work this out in your head: one thousand... plus forty...

LOUISE. Answer me, April.

APRIL. Plus a thousand...

LOUISE. April!

APRIL. Plus thirty…

LOUISE. April!

22. 20 June 1984, Paris

Métro

DECEMBER (*taking a photo out of his pocket*). Look. Told you she was beautiful.

GERARD. Another beautician, eh?

DECEMBER. Engineer, actually.

GERARD (*doubtful*). Really. Her?

DECEMBER. Specialises in designing safes.

GERARD (*after a pause*)….Does she now?

DECEMBER. For banks, big banks.
   …She'll probably never call me.

23. 23 June 1984, Paris

Telephone

The telephone rings. DECEMBER *answers.*

DECEMBER. Hello?

APRIL. December?

DECEMBER….April?

APRIL. Are you free this evening? And if so, do you have a car? Can you pick me up at eight?

DECEMBER. Er…

APRIL. You haven't got a car?

DECEMBER. …I have, I have a car.

APRIL. Oh, maybe you were planning on watching the match?

DECEMBER. No, no, not at all…

APRIL. Are you sure? We could do another… [time.]

DECEMBER. No. This evening is fine

Enter GERARD.

GERARD. You're kidding me.

DECEMBER. Sorry, Gerard.

GERARD. France-Portugal, the European Championship
Semi-Final!
Two games away from making history!

DECEMBER. We'll go another day!

GERARD. Championship only happens every four years, idiot!

Enter LOUISE.

LOUISE. You're joking, right?

APRIL. Sorry, Louise.

LOUISE. Bailing on the Renoir retrospective, again!

APRIL. There's more to life than films!

DECEMBER. So, that being said, er, your car…

GERARD. What about my car?

DECEMBER. You won't be using it?

GERARD. Are you for real?

LOUISE. You want to show him your bank?

GERARD. She wants to show you her bank?

DECEMBER. I didn't catch it all. She wants to see me again,
that's the main thing.

APRIL. I'll explain later. So do you want to come?

DECEMBER. Gerard, will you lend me your car or not?

GERARD. Urmm... how about NO!

LOUISE (*sighing*). And if François asks, you were with me, right?

24. 23 June 1984, 8.24 p.m., Paris

France-Portugal

A loud horn blows. It could be a foghorn.
APRIL and DECEMBER are in GERARD's car, stuck in
a traffic jam.

DECEMBER....So where is it exactly?

APRIL. Boulevard des Italiens. Near Opéra.

Sounds coming from a café on their right can be heard.
A huge cheer goes up.
DECEMBER switches on the radio.

THE RADIO (*voice-over*). Goal! Domergue with a classy free kick, straight past Bento who was rooted to the spot. France one, Portugal nil.

DECEMBER switches off the radio.

APRIL. We're winning, you should be pleased.

DECEMBER. I don't care, I was just checking the traffic.

APRIL. Okay then.

DECEMBER. Who was that book for?

APRIL. For you.

DECEMBER. No, seriously.

APRIL. For you.

DECEMBER (*shaking his head*). Okay, and did you read it or...?

APRIL. No. Go back to your story, when did he become a magician?

DECEMBER. He suddenly got the urge fifteen years later.

APRIL. You told me he made clocks.

DECEMBER. Yes, clocks. And automatons, in a small workshop in Belleville...

APRIL. So what changed?

DECEMBER.... Because he met another woman, alright!

APRIL. Younger?

DECEMBER. Obviously.

APRIL. Pretty?

DECEMBER. I don't know. I wasn't there!

25. 17 May 1844, Paris

Wineseller

JEAN. Margot? Margot?

JEAN-EUGÈNE ROBERT-HOUDIN *is now aged thirty-eight.* MARGOT, *his new wife, is twenty-five.*

MARGOT. Jean, I've worked it out, that trick yesterday. You used a string attached to your wrist to make the little scarf disappear, didn't you?

JEAN (*kissing her*). Absolutely not.
(*Leaving again.*) I'm going back to the workshop.

MARGOT. And dinner?

JEAN. I won't be long.

MARGOT. Get some wine on your way back?

JEAN. Yes, my love.

MARGOT. Not from the wine store you went to yesterday.
    It was corked.

JEAN. Okay.

MARGOT. Go to the one next to the butcher's.

JEAN. The butcher's.

MARGOT. No, not the butcher's, the baker's?

JEAN. The baker's.

MARGOT. Or the butcher's?

JEAN (*teasing her*). Or the candlestick maker's?

MARGOT. Stop it. You know, the one with the red shop front…

JEAN. I don't know.

MARGOT.…in the lane, what was the name… leading off the
    high street? The one with cobblestones.

JEAN. I'll find it!

MARGOT. Red front!

THE ANTIQUES DEALER. Jean-Eugène Robert-Houdin set
    off to look for a wineseller's with a red shop front and
    quickly got lost in the tiny mediaeval streets of Paris.
    Jean passed a boutique that he had never noticed before.
    An antiques shop.
    He stopped to look in the window.
    There were a few bits of old furniture, the odd painting.
    And in the middle of this muddle…

JEAN. No.

THE WATCHMAKER. He rubbed his eyes as if to see better.

JEAN. Impossible.

THE WATCHMAKER. He told himself that it must be a copy…
He went in, not daring to believe it could be true.

26. The Antiques Dealer

JEAN *enters the shop*.
THE WATCHMAKER *has turned into* THE ANTIQUES
DEALER.

JEAN (*to* THE ANTIQUES DEALER). Excuse me…

THE ANTIQUES DEALER. Come in, come in. Look all you
want. No pressure to buy. I've also got toys as well if you
have children.

JEAN. That automaton over there behind the cupboard, is it the
original one?

THE ANTIQUES DEALER. Not for sale.

JEAN (*slowly approaching*). I thought it had been destroyed in
a fire…

THE ANTIQUES DEALER. I repeat, not for sale, Mr Robert-
Houdin.

JEAN (*turning slowly towards* THE ANTIQUES DEALER).
How do you know my name?

THE ANTIQUES DEALER. I know your automatons.

JEAN (*pointing to* THE ANTIQUES DEALER*'s automaton*).
That one is a pure marvel.
I can offer you ten thousand francs for it.

THE ANTIQUES DEALER (*sighing*). That's quite a sum. But
there's no point you getting into debt like that.

THE ANTIQUES DEALER *moves towards the shop door.*

JEAN. Why?

THE ANTIQUES DEALER (*locking the door*). The automaton belonged to my father, and without him, it's useless.

JEAN. Your father?

THE ANTIQUES DEALER. It's a good story but it takes a long time to tell.
Do you have the time?

JEAN. Of course.

THE ANTIQUES DEALER *invites* JEAN *to sit down*.

The following story should also visually be brought to life by the chorus of actors .

THE ANTIQUES DEALER. Well, the story begins in 1776 in the powerful Republic of the Two Nations, Ukraine and Poland, which had just been divided by Imperial Russia. But in the fortified town of Riga, a revolt broke out, led by a Polish rebel called Worousky.

He was not particularly tall nor particularly strong, but he was a very skilful strategist. The rebels initially had the upper hand. Then the Russians sent in reinforcements.

During the battle, Worousky took a bullet in each leg. But still managed to hide in a makeshift shelter. When night fell, he slowly and painfully dragged himself through enemy territory in search of a doctor who wasn't Russian. Completely exhausted, he miraculously ended up knocking on the door of Dr Johann Von Kempelen.

An Austrian doctor, inventor and, above all, a humanist. Von Kempelen hid the rebel, diagnosing gangrene in both legs, and immediately amputating them. Worousky was unconscious for several days, hovering between life and death. Then he woke up.

The two couldn't speak the other's language.

And the loss of his legs cast Warousky into a deep depression. He refused to eat, slowly starving himself to death.

Then one day Von Kempelen placed a chessboard between them. Worousky took a few minutes to learn the rules and only a few hours to beat Von Kempelen. Worousky won time and time again: his skill as a strategist made him virtually unbeatable.

He started eating again, built up his strength, and that was the beginning of the unlikely friendship between an Austrian doctor and a Polish rebel.

At this point the Russians stepped up their house-to-house searches. The noose was tightening. Several times Worousky urged his host to give him up. Von Kempelen categorically refused.

Instead, in less than three months, he put together his masterpiece: it was a low, medium-sized cabinet, which contained a complex mechanism. On top of the cabinet was a chessboard.

When Worousky first saw it, he didn't understand what it was for. Von Kempelen invited his friend to get into the secret compartment just the right size for someone with no legs. For the very first time Worousky became the Mechanical Turk.

The two friends tested the deception on a neighbour first. He was thoroughly beaten. A second tried his luck, then a third.

The Mechanical Turk beat them all.

Von Kempelen spent time perfecting his sales pitch; Worousky practised his robotic movements. Finally they planned a route for Worousky to escape, and stopped in each town along the way to present the Turk.

As they moved towards the Polish border, their success outstripped all their expectations. People fought, and paid, to be able to watch or measure their skill against this fantastic chess-playing automaton.

By the time they arrived in Vitebsk, word had even reached Empress Catherine II of Russia, she invited them to perform in St Petersburg.

Freedom was only a few miles away. The border. But the idea of duping Catherine the Great was just too tempting...

They turned back and headed to the Russian court.

Worousky the rebel was sitting opposite his worst enemy, the Mother of the Nation, Empress Catherine II of Russia, also a formidable chess player.

On realising that she was losing the game, the Empress made a forbidden move. Nobody said a word. Worousky slowly lifted the offending chess piece and put it back in its original position.

In a total of eleven moves, he checkmated her.

Catherine took her defeat well. Congratulating Von Kempelen on his marvellous invention.

After that the two men visited and performed in the greatest courts of Europe for years, and grew considerably wealthier.

When Worousky eventually retired, he married a Frenchwoman, had several children, of whom I am the eldest.

You must understand that without my father inside it, the machine will be of no use to you at all.

27. 18 May 1844, Paris

Theatre

JEAN *has returned home and just told his wife the story.*

JEAN. A man with no legs wearing a disguise, Margot!

THE ANTIQUES DEALER. There's a lesson to be learnt from this story. A magician can't help but turn anything into something magical. Even an automaton.

JEAN. The greatest courts of Europe, Margot!
An Austrian doctor and a Pole with no legs.

The doctor would have spent his whole life in that small town if he hadn't met the wounded Pole! And the Pole would have been shot if he hadn't met...

MARGOT. A magician.

JEAN (*smiling*). They went on the road. Made a fortune. (*Sighing.*) The greatest courts of Europe...

MARGOT. Go for it, Jean.

JEAN (*coming out of his reverie*). What did you say?

MARGOT. You don't need to meet a man with no legs to become a great magician.

JEAN. Me? Margot, I'm thirty-eight years old.

MARGOT. Is there an age limit?

Your first marriage, you did the responsible thing for your family. You rightly relegated your life as an artiste to a corner of your memory. Built clocks for fifteen years. But today your first wife is no longer with us. And I don't need you to build clocks.
I suggest you live an adventure.

JEAN. You may dream about a bohemian life, but when you find yourself in a caravan, rain pouring down, drumming up business in a village square, believe me, you'll regret you ever left your Paris.

MARGOT. Then forget the caravan. Buy a theatre.

JEAN. A theatre?

MARGOT. Why not? New places open every week in 'my' Paris!

JEAN (*beginning to be tempted*). But what would I present?

MARGOT. A show! Your show!
The illusions you've invented, every day, for the past fifteen years, with the automatons you've designed, every day, for the past fifteen years.

JEAN. I've yet to invent the trick that'll make enough money appear to buy a theatre.

MARGOT. Let's sell the workshop!

JEAN. If a craftsman could sell his workshop and have enough to buy a theatre, there wouldn't be many craftsmen left in Paris...

MARGOT. Then buy a shop! An apartment! A cellar!
Turn it into a theatre. It'd be a small theatre. But it'd be *your* theatre.

JEAN (*starting to be convinced*). Everything would have to be built...

MARGOT. Yes!

JEAN....the stalls, the lighting, the auditorium...

MARGOT. Yes!

JEAN....mirrors, pullies, cables, trapdoors for disappearing acts would have to be put in!
Is that the life you really want, Margot? An artiste's life?

MARGOT (*smiling*). The greatest courts of Europe, Jean.

JEAN....A small theatre?

MARGOT. A very small theatre. Two hundred seats, no more.

28. 23 June 1984, 9.29 p.m., Paris

BNP

APRIL *and* DECEMBER *are in the bank on Boulevard des Italiens.*

DECEMBER. Why exactly are we here?

APRIL. It's the Banque Nationale de Paris head office.

DECEMBER. Yes.

APRIL. It's where I work.

DECEMBER. I know that, but why...

A TV (*voice-over*). Chalana crosses into the box it finds
    Jordão's head, and Jordão scores! One all.

MANUEL (*in a Portuguese accent*). Yes! Yes!! GOAAALLL!!

DECEMBER. Who to?

MANUEL. PORTUGAL! One–all.

DECEMBER. Really! One–all. (Not that I care.)

APRIL. December, this is Manuel, security. Manuel supports…

MANUEL. PORTUGAL!

APRIL. Manuel, you don't mind if we visit the vault, do you?

MANUEL. The vault or the basement?

APRIL. Just the vault.

MANUEL (*euphoric*). Yes, yes, go ahead! Goal! Goal!

DECEMBER (*still thinking about the match*). Shit, shit, shit…

APRIL. The vault is currently being renovated. The demolition
    bit is over. Building begins tomorrow.

*They enter the vault, torches in hand. They look around
    them. The walls are bare.*

DECEMBER. I've got a bad feeling about the…

APRIL. About the match?

DECEMBER. No, about the vault.

APRIL. Right. Well no need to be scared.

The building itself dates from the 1920s. However, under the
    vault, there was a layer of concrete, which was dug up. Are
    you actually listening?

DECEMBER. Yep, yep.

APRIL. And under that layer of concrete, there was a floor
    dating back to before the building was constructed.

DECEMBER (*trying to focus*). Okay.

APRIL. In a corner of the room, we found a small slab of marble. I had them lift up the slab.

Underneath there was a spiral staircase. Which led down to a room that wasn't in their plans.

DECEMBER. What?

APRIL. I had them lift up the slab of marble, because there was an inscription on the wall…

APRIL *shines her torch on the inscription:*
'Théâtre Robert-Houdin
Public entrance'

DECEMBER (*flabbergasted*). Holy shit. Can we see it?

APRIL. No, it's not safe and Manuel has the keys.

DECEMBER (*pulling out a bunch of keys from his pocket*).
…You mean these?

APRIL *looks at* DECEMBER *and smiles.*

29. 1844–1984, Paris

Crypt

THE ANTIQUES DEALER *is showing* JEAN *around.*

THE ANTIQUES DEALER. It's an old crypt, built in the late sixteenth century by the Bourbon-Montpensiers.

JEAN. It's very deep down.

DECEMBER. It's deep down, isn't it?

APRIL. Very. We're probably the first to come in here since the building was razed to the ground.

DECEMBER. So you bought the book because you saw the inscription?

THE ANTIQUES DEALER. Only empty because people say between the time it was built and the fall of the monarchy, this cellar was the backdrop to several black masses and other satanic practices. You'd be silly to let that put you off.

JEAN. It's dark.

DECEMBER. It's dark.

APRIL.... It's a cellar.

THE ANTIQUES DEALER. Hence the price is very low.

JEAN. It'll need a lot of work.

THE ANTIQUES DEALER (*playing down that aspect*). Cosmetic mainly...

JEAN. It'll take time... a year, maybe more.

THE ANTIQUES DEALER. Nah, eight months, at the most.

JEAN. But what better home for a sorcerer than a place where sorcery has been practised?

THE ANTIQUES DEALER. Yeah... why not.

JEAN ponders for a moment or two, then says:

JEAN. Ladies and gentlemen, welcome to this theatre.

30. 1845, Théâtre Robert-Houdin, Paris

Fantastic Evening

Robert-Houdin's first 'fantastic evening'.
JEAN performs several tricks.
He makes scarves, then a bunch of flowers appear...
He makes a walking stick fly through the air. He makes
MARGOT levitate and then disappear.
He disappears in turn in a cloud of smoke...

31. 23 June 1984, 9.40 p.m., Paris

Théâtre Robert-Houdin

The smoke clears and APRIL *and* DECEMBER *are seen in the cellar.*

DECEMBER. Honestly, I'm a little disappointed.

APRIL. What were you expecting? A magic show?

DECEMBER. I don't know. That we'd find automatons? Or something. But it's a cellar. It's just a cellar.

APRIL. A hundred years later, obviously.
I think a bomb must have fallen on it during the war… why the entrance was blocked up.

DECEMBER. We just have to imagine it… full every evening. Whenever he performed, the show was sold out.
He employed eight musicians. Famous across the globe.

APRIL. When did he die?

DECEMBER. 1870, I think.
Hey, look!
(*He shines his torch on an inscription.*)
'Robert-Houdin, 1805 to 1871.'

APRIL. And after him, did the theatre close?

DECEMBER. No, no, it was taken over.
I don't know by who, but it was taken over.

32. 1883, Paris

Georges

Young GEORGES *has grown up. He's now twenty-two.*
THE PAINTER *is none other than* THE WATCHMAKER.
He holds a brush in his hand and turns towards the canvas.

THE PAINTER. I just have one question to ask you, Georges: why do you want to paint?

GEORGES. I'm not completely sure. All I know is that I wasn't made to be a bootmaker.

THE PAINTER. What does your father think about that?

GEORGES. I work part-time in the factory, repairing machines mainly.

THE PAINTER.... You're very clever with your hands, it seems.

GEORGES. I like mechanics, yes, but not as much as painting.

THE PAINTER. So why not go to art school?

GEORGES (*after a pause*). My father won't allow me to.
I want to paint because I have so many things to express, you see, and I'm convinced that one can express infinitely more with an image than with words.

THE PAINTER (*after a pause*)....Suzanne!

Enter SUZANNE. *She's seventeen.*

Suzanne, this is Georges. I'm going to give him a few painting lessons.
Georges, this is Suzanne. I'd like you to start by painting her portrait.
Is that alright with you Georges?
...Georges?

33. 1883, Paris

Suzanne

SUZANNE. Mr Georges, you're not being serious!

GEORGES. Suzanne, the world is already far too serious, why should we be too? Don't you like my kisses?

SUZANNE. Yes, but...

GEORGES (*taking her by the waist*). Don't you trust me?

SUZANNE. Yes, but Mr Georges…

GEORGES. Please stop calling me 'mister'!

SUZANNE. Alright. But Mr Georges, you come from a well-respected family and…

GEORGES (*ironic*). A well-respected family of shoemakers, no sorry, I meant bootmakers!

SUZANNE. I'm just a caretaker's daughter.

GEORGES. Not just. You want to be an actress!

SUZANNE. Again. You're not being serious…

GEORGES. I am serious! And I want to get married…

SUZANNE. No!

GEORGES.…I am asking you solemnly: Suzanne, will you be my wife?

SUZANNE (*for a moment very moved, then shaking her head*). Mr Georges, you are too kind. But your father would never agree.

GEORGES. My father has a heart, Suzanne. I'm going to tell him that I'm in love with my muse, in love with a future great actress, a budding Sarah Bernhardt, an Ophelia, a Marianne, a Juliet! How could he refuse?

34. 1884, Paris

A Caretaker's Daughter

LOUIS. Are you joking, Georges? A caretaker's daughter?

CATHERINE. Georges, answer your father when he speaks to you.

LOUIS. As long as I'm alive you will not marry that girl!

CATHERINE. Go on, answer him!

LOUIS (*to* CATHERINE). Fine. To England with you, he can work selling shoes. Only way he'll forget her, Catherine.

GEORGES. To England?

LOUIS. A year or two, three even, if that's what it takes, but he will forget her.

CATHERINE.... To England?

LOUIS. To England!

35. 1884, London

England

GEORGES *has just got off the ferry.*

WILLIAM. Master George! Master George!
  How do you do? I'm Master William Higgins. But call me Willy. Everyone calls me Willy. I work for your parents. Is that all your luggage?

GEORGES (*not understanding*). *Comment?* What?

WILLIAM (*pointing to his suitcase*). Luggage, er... *baggage*?

GEORGES. Ah, yes, yes!

WILLIAM (*picking up his suitcase and speaking slowly*).
  Spiffing! We're lucky it's not raining!

GEORGES. What?

WILLIAM. Raining!

GEORGES. Ah raining, yes. Lucky.

The sky rumbles and it starts to rain.

WILLIAM (*with enthusiasm*).... Well, welcome to London.

36. 1884, London

Shop

THE CUSTOMER (*angry*). Who on earth sent me this first-class fool?

GEORGES (*with a strong French accent*). Pardon, madam.

WILLIAM. Whatever did he do wrong?

THE CUSTOMER. What did he do right? I asked for French high-heeled shoes and he brought me Italian low-heeled shoes.

GEORGES. Sorry.

WILLIAM. I apologise unreservedly, madam, he's new to the shop I'm afraid.

THE CUSTOMER. Sure he's not new to the world?

WILLIAM (*taking the customer with him*). Let me assist you, madam.
Georges, oddly, you're not very good in the shoe department. So let's see how you get on selling ladies' undergarments.

GEORGES. What?

WILLIAM. Lingerie, corsets...

GEORGES. Lingerie? Me?

WILLIAM. *Oui*. But please tell them you're French first.
(*On the way out.*)
Then the ladies won't mind if you can't speak a word of English.
Will you be joining us in pub later, Georges?

GEORGES (*to* SUZANNE). No thank you, Willy. I have to write to my fiancée.

WILLIAM. Marvellous. Write a fantastic letter, then!

37.

Love Letters

GEORGES. 'Suzanne, my love. It rains all the time here and they drink a lot of tea. I miss you terribly. The touch of your skin, your smile, your caresses, the sound of your voice.'

SUZANNE. 'Mr Georges…'

GEORGES. 'I'm trying hard to be the worst possible salesman, so I'll get fired and return to you sooner.'

SUZANNE. 'Mr Georges…'

GEORGES. 'I long to see you again. Take you to the theatre, cover you with kisses, marry you.'

SUZANNE. 'Georges!
I received all your letters.
I miss you, too. A lot.
But your father came to see me. He talked with me, convinced me. I'm not meant to be part of your world.'

GEORGES. 'Suzanne, don't listen to my father. I've decided to marry you without his permission. We're going to get married and be very happy.'

SUZANNE. 'Georges, I've met someone else.
His name is Lucien. He's studying at an elite institute in Paris. Great prospects, same age as me and he wants to marry me too…
Please don't write to me any more.'

38. 1885, London

Pub

At the pub.

WILLIAM. Here, old fella, another beer for you.
Why so glum? You know what they say in French: *Une de
perdue, dix tu retrouves…* [*There are plenty more fish in the
sea… (literally: 'One lost, ten found.')*]

No reaction.

By Jove, gentlemen who are unlucky in love have done some
of the most amazing things in the world. Think of Shakespeare!

GEORGES. Shakespeare was a genius.

WILLIAM. I started photography after getting my heart broken.
Do you know about photography?

GEORGES. Yes, yes I do.

WILLIAM. Marvellous! I'll show you my studio one day.
Let's do something to take your mind off things – (*Taking
him by the arm.*)
Do you enjoy magic?

GEORGES. Magic?

WILLIAM. Magic! Have you ever seen a magic show?

GEORGES *shakes his head.*

Never? Right, let's go then!

39. 1886, Paris

Attic

CATHERINE. Georges?

> GEORGES, *alone, stands facing the audience, a pack of cards in his hand. He lives in the attic of the building on Boulevard Saint-Martin.*

> (*Entering.*) Georges?

GEORGES. Ah, Mother, you've come just at the right time. Think of a card.

CATHERINE. Georges, you haven't been downstairs since yesterday...

GEORGES. The queen of hearts? Very well.

CATHERINE. Since your father died, you've hardly left this attic.

> *The queen of hearts pops up in* GEORGES' *pack of cards.*

GEORGES. Another trick?

CATHERINE. These tricks! That stupid pack of cards is all that you brought back from London.

GEORGES. Aren't you satisfied? What more can I do, Mother? Suzanne has left me, I repair the machines, and I live with you.

CATHERINE. Grow up, Georges, grow up a little.
Go out, take over the factory, do what you want with it, but do something!

> *Exit* CATHERINE.
> GEORGES *remains alone, in the middle of the attic.*
> *And time moves on to 1887, then...*

40. 1888, Paris

The Antiques Dealer

GEORGES *is twenty-seven when he, in turn, enters* THE ANTIQUES DEALER's *shop*

THE ANTIQUES DEALER. Come in, come in, sir! You can look all you want. No pressure to buy.

GEORGES (*entering the shop*). Tell me, that automaton over there, is it...

THE ANTIQUES DEALER. The original, yes, but it's not for sale, Georges.

GEORGES *looks at* THE ANTIQUES DEALER *in astonishment.*

I saw you perform the other night at the Chat Noir. You're a magician.

GEORGES....An amateur. I've lots of free time.

THE ANTIQUES DEALER. Time is a rare commodity.

GEORGES. My father made boots, my grandfather made boots...

THE ANTIQUES DEALER....And you make magic.

GEORGES (*sighing*). And I paint. And take photographs.

THE ANTIQUES DEALER. Well, well! Is that all?

GEORGES. No, I also write inferior poetry and compose very very mediocre music...
My only success is I managed to inherit a factory.

THE ANTIQUES DEALER. Your turn will come, Georges.

GEORGES. What did you say?

THE ANTIQUES DEALER. Need to close the shop for a while. I have a delivery to make to a theatre.

GEORGES. A theatre? Which theatre?

THE ANTIQUES DEALER. Just the one underneath, a
   curiosity, a former crypt, built in the late sixteenth century...
   Would you like to come with me?

GEORGES. I should already be home by now.

THE ANTIQUES DEALER (*not listening to him*). It's been
   somewhat neglected since the death of its owner, Mr Robert-
   Houdin.
   Anyhow, I bid you good evening.

GEORGES. Wait! I beg your pardon. Who?

41. 1888, Paris

Théâtre Robert-Houdin

THE ANTIQUES DEALER *enters the theatre, followed by*
GEORGES, *who is carrying a box.*

THE ANTIQUES DEALER. My friends, this is an apprentice
   magician who kindly helped me carry my boxes.
   (*To* GEORGES.) Just put that down there!
   Thank you, once again.

GEORGES (*discovering where he is*). But... it's just a cellar!

THE ANTIQUES DEALER. Quite right. Let me introduce you
   to the troupe.

GEORGES. I mean that...

THE ANTIQUES DEALER. Marius, stage manager and
   comedian.

GEORGES. How do you do!

THE ANTIQUES DEALER. This is Trouillet, the pianist...

GEORGES. Hello!

THE ANTIQUES DEALER. Madame Gabrielle, the cashier…

GEORGES (*extending his hand to be shaken, but she ignores it*). How do you do!

THE ANTIQUES DEALER. Ah, and here's our leading lady, specialising in conjuring tricks, Suzanne.

GEORGES *turns round to see* SUZANNE, *now twenty-three*.

SUZANNE.…Mr Georges.

GEORGES. Suzanne.

THE ANTIQUES DEALER. Did I mention that the theatre was for sale?

42. 23 June 1984, 9.47 p.m., Paris

Georges

DECEMBER. Georges.

APRIL. What?

DECEMBER (*shining his torch*). The last director was called Georges.
It's written there.

APRIL. Georges what?

43. 1889, Paris

Safe

A year later.

MARIUS. Sir! Sir!

GEORGES. Ah, Marius. The machinery made much too much noise. Trouillet will have to play the piano louder! (*He hands his jacket to* SUZANNE.) Thank you, Suzanne.

MARIUS. I'll tell him, but...

GEORGES. How's the work coming along?

MARIUS. Quite well, but...

GEORGES. And the audience? Madame Gabrielle, how many people were in the audience yesterday? Thirty?

MADAME GABRIELLE. Eighteen.

GEORGES. Eighteen, in a theatre that seats...?

MADAME GABRIELLE. Two hundred.

GEORGES (*stoically*). Two hundred.

MARIUS (*playing it down*). One hundred and ninety actually. We've found something, sir. Hidden behind a wall light.

GEORGES. What?

MARIUS. A safe.

GEORGES. A safe?

MARIUS. A safety deposit box.

GEORGES. Have you opened it?

MARIUS. No, not really. Come and see.
There's something written on the outside.

MADAME GABRIELLE. 'When Vaucanson made a duck.'

MARIUS. That's it.

GEORGES (*reading*). 'When Vaucanson made a duck.'
That must be the code to open the safe.

MARIUS. Yes, but to open the safe you need numbers.

GEORGES. It's a riddle.
Jacques de Vaucanson was a watchmaker.
He built an extraordinary automaton, a mechanical duck,
which could quack, swim, eat, drink and…

MADAME GABRIELLE. And?

GEORGES (*searching for the right word*)….excrete.

SUZANNE. And what year was that?

GEORGES. In 1738, it was in 1738.
One, seven, three, eight, Marius.

MARIUS. One, seven, three, eight.

MADAME GABRIELLE. In 1738?

GEORGES. It must have been a trick, of some sort.

MARIUS. It works!

MARIUS *takes a medium-sized box out of the safe.*

MADAME GABRIELLE (*circumspect*). A box.

GEORGES (*reading*). 'Life is a circle.'

SUZANNE (*reading*). 'By Jean-Eugène Robert-Houdin.'

GEORGES. It's a sign. The audience will return, Madame
Gabrielle. We're going to bring this theatre back to life.

GEORGES *opens the tin.*

MADAME GABRIELLE. What's in it?

MARIUS. It's a wax cylinder.

GEORGES (*with wide-open eyes*). Find me a phonograph.

MARIUS. A what?

GEORGES. The voice of Robert-Houdin is on this.
Find me a phonograph.

44. 23 June 1984, 9.49 p.m., Paris

Safe

DECEMBER. There's a safe here.

APRIL.... What?

DECEMBER (*shining his torch on the wall*). It's hidden behind a fixture, set into the wall, but there's definitely a safe here.

APRIL. There's a safe within a safe?

DECEMBER (*his excitement growing*). This is your speciality, isn't it?

APRIL. I suppose.

DECEMBER. Can you open it?

APRIL. Of course.

DECEMBER. How long will it take you?

APRIL. Less than five minutes.

DECEMBER. Seriously?

APRIL. It's an 1849 Lauzier with a dual safety mechanism. (*She cracks her fingers.*)
Bring me the toolbox that's behind you, and get out your stopwatch.

45. 28 December 1895, Paris

Mr Antoine

GEORGES *is seated on the edge of the stage.*
SUZANNE *comes up behind him.*

THE WATCHMAKER (*off*). Some believe that life is a straight line.
But life is a circle, since we're all turning.
It's an eternal recommencement.

Knowing when it will be your turn is the only question.
Come in, Georges. Come closer.

GEORGES. How do you know my name?

THE WATCHMAKER (*off*). I know a lot of things.

SUZANNE.…people will come eventually, Mr Georges.

GEORGES. Thank you, Suzanne.
(*He sighs.*)
Unfortunately, after five years spent waiting for them, I think
we can safely say that people won't come.
I've tried everything. Renovating the theatre, presenting new
tricks, putting big names on the bill… How did Robert-
Houdin do it? The house was full every night.

SUZANNE. It was a different era.

GEORGES *turns towards* SUZANNE.

GEORGES. You wanted to tell me something?

SUZANNE (*after several moments' hesitation*). I've been
offered a role at the Renaissance.
(*Savouring the irony of it.*)
Playing opposite Sarah Bernhardt.

GEORGES (*struggling to hide his disappointment*). The
Renaissance! My goodness! That's a step up in the world!

SUZANNE. It's only a few lines.
Georges, thank you. For these past five years. You could
have dismissed me for no reason; I wouldn't even have held
it against you. But you kept me on, without ever being
disrespectful and…

GEORGES. What happened to your suitor? The handsome
young man with the good prospects?

SUZANNE (*after a pause*). Why did you buy this theatre,
Georges?

GEORGES. I wanted to marry you. I couldn't. So I had to find
some way of staying close to you. But you're right to leave.
The theatre will be closing soon.

SUZANNE. Why's that?

GEORGES. I sold my shares in the family business.

SUZANNE. You didn't!

GEORGES.... If I hadn't, we would have shut down a long time ago.

She comes and sits beside him.

I would have liked to have been so many things...
Would have liked to have invented an extraordinary illusion that would have filled the theatre every night, and covered me in glory in your eyes.
But I'm thirty-four and I haven't invented anything.
I will always just be the son of a bootmaker.

THE ANTIQUES DEALER (*entering*). Georges?

GEORGES. Mr Antoine?

THE ANTIQUES DEALER. Am I disturbing you? I let myself in...

GEORGES. Not at all. Do you know Suzanne?

THE ANTIQUES DEALER. 'The disappearing lady', of course. Tell me, what are you both doing tonight?

GEORGES. Us? Tonight?

THE ANTIQUES DEALER. If your curiosity tempts you, come and see what's on at the Grand Café.

GEORGES. The Grand Café?

THE ANTIQUES DEALER. That's right.
My sons are preparing an experiment that might interest you.
At eight p.m. Come as my guests.

GEORGES. You've got children? I didn't know that!

THE ANTIQUES DEALER (*leaving the stage*).... Eight p.m. at the Grand Café!

GEORGES. Would you like to go? Unless you're seeing...

SUZANNE....Lucien?

GEORGES. Lucien.

SUZANNE (*smiling*). I left him. Last month.

46. 28 December 1895, 8 p.m., Paris

Grand Café

At the Grand Café, 14 Boulevard des Capucines, Paris.

THE ANTIQUES DEALER. Great, you came!
   (*Going towards them.*)
   This way.

GEORGES. To the basement?

THE ANTIQUES DEALER. The Indian Room in the basement.
   Actually it's a cellar. Volpini rents it to me for thirty francs a
   day. I offered him twenty per cent of the takings but he
   didn't want to know.

GEORGES. How much is the admission?

THE ANTIQUES DEALER....One franc. For you both it's free.

GEORGES. And how long does the 'experiment' last?

THE ANTIQUES DEALER. Not even half an hour.
   Here, take a seat.

   SUZANNE *and* GEORGES *sit down and look around them.*

SUZANNE. Thirty people. Hardly a crowd.

GEORGES. It's a premiere.

SUZANNE (*turning around*). What's that machine?

GEORGES (*turning around*)....It looks like a magic lantern.
   Nothing out of the ordinary.

47. Paris, 23 June 1984, 9.53 p.m.

In the Safe

DECEMBER. Four minutes.

APRIL. Don't distract me.

DECEMBER. Four minutes and five seconds.
If I wanted to distract you, I'd tell you that you were the
most beautiful woman that I'd ever met. Clever, too.
(*Remembering*.) And engaged. And pregnant.

A muffled noise is heard. APRIL *has opened the safe.*

APRIL. How long?

DECEMBER. Four minutes, twenty-five seconds.

APRIL. Punctual, too. I'm very punctual.

She leans inside the safe, helped by DECEMBER *shining the
torch. She takes out a circular tin. A film tin.*

48. 28 December 1895 – 23 June 1984

Lumière

The Arrival of a Train at La Ciotat Station *begins.*
The first public film screening.
*The images come alive. One can hear the train whistling,
moving along the rails.*
Then come colours. The image grows larger.
The music grows louder.
*More than a hundred years of moving pictures flash across the
screen in a few seconds.*
*The music grows louder and louder, then suddenly stops, as the
lights come on again abruptly.*

GEORGES (*standing up, utterly flabbergasted*). Stupendous!
It's stupendous!
I'll give you one thousand francs for it right now!

THE ANTIQUES DEALER. It's pointless.

DECEMBER (*looking inside the tin*). A reel of film!

GEORGES. Two thousand francs… five thousand francs!

THE ANTIQUES DEALER. Don't tire yourself.

SUZANNE. Georges.

GEORGES. Ten thousand francs… ten thousand francs for your machine! Does it have a name, at least?

DECEMBER. There's something written on the tin…

THE ANTIQUES DEALER. The director of the Musée Grévin has already just offered me twenty thousand francs for it.

LALLEMENT. And I'll give you fifty thousand!

Exclamations from the public.

SUZANNE. That's the director of the Folies Bergères music hall.

LALLEMENT. Can anyone top that?

THE ANTIQUES DEALER. Gentlemen, gentlemen, it's pointless, really… This invention is not for sale and, believe me, I'm saving all of you from bankruptcy. It'll be shown for a while, like a scientific curiosity, but commercially speaking, there's no future in it.

GEORGES. Come on, Suzanne, let's go!

They leave, excited and scowling at the same time.

DECEMBER. 'Star Films present…'

LALLEMENT. Who's that young man in such a hurry?

THE ANTIQUES DEALER. Don't you know Georges? The heir to Méliès Boots.

DECEMBER. '…a film by Georges Méliès'.

THE ANTIQUES DEALER.…A name to remember.

49. 23 June 1984, 9.54 p.m., Paris

Méliès

APRIL. Méliès!
A Méliès film, here?!

DECEMBER. It was him!
He was the last director of the Théâtre Robert-Houdin.
Georges Méliès!

APRIL. We're holding a Méliès film in our hands!

DECEMBER. Yes, but we don't know which film it is; there's
no title. It's probably one that everyone has already seen.

APRIL. But what if it's one nobody has ever seen?

DECEMBER. Yes, but what if they have?

APRIL. We have to find out! We have to watch this film!

DECEMBER. But to watch this film, we have to steal it, get
past Manuel and find a nineteenth-century projector that still
works!

APRIL. Great! First things first, how are we going to get past
Manuel?

DECEMBER (*after a pause*). Time to show you how good I am
at my job…

50. 28 December 1895, Paris

The Perfect Illusion

SUZANNE *and* GEORGES *are outside, exultant*.

GEORGES. That's it! The perfect illusion! That is it!
The future of the theatre, magic, entertainment!
Suzanne, I must get that machine!

SUZANNE. But, Georges, they don't want to sell it.

GEORGES (*feeling exhilarated*). So we'll have to build one.

SUZANNE. Nobody in France knows how to.

GEORGES. Oh no, I'll have to go back to England.

51. 23 June 1984, 9.58 p.m., Paris

Goal

THE TV (*voice-over*). And Chalana passes it to Jordão who catches it in mid-air and puts it in the back of the net!

MANUEL. Bravo! BRAVO, Portugal!

THE TV (*voice-over*). What a devastating blow for France! In the ninety-eighth minute, right in the middle of extra time, Portugal now two goals to one!

APRIL. Manuel?

MANUEL. Goal, Miss April, a goal for Portugal!

APRIL *gestures to* DECEMBER *to creep past without being seen.*

THE TV (*voice-over*). Time is running out for France to find a way back into this game.

DECEMBER *creeps by, head low, with the film under his shirt.*
He steals a glance at the match on TV all the same.

APRIL. Really? Aaah... who scored?

MANUEL. Jordão, again!

DECEMBER. Oh shit!

APRIL. Again!! He's great at kicking... and scoring.

MANUEL. Ha, ha! Football's not really your thing, is it? You prefer films, don't you?

APRIL. Not at all. I'm kinda into football!

MANUEL. And where's your friend?

APRIL (*panicking*). Well actually, Manuel, I've always needed someone…. someone to explain what that rule is about being offside?

52. January 1896, Paris

Kinetograph

MARIUS. I don't understand, boss. Why would you go to England to buy a prototype of an image machine?

GEORGES. I've got an English friend, Willy errm William, he's a photography buff. I'm going to buy his machine and the shots he's taken.

MADAME GABRIELLE. For how much?

GEORGES. I'll offer him one thousand francs for the lot.

MADAME GABRIELLE. One thousand…

MARIUS. And you go tomorrow?

GEORGES. Yes, tomorrow. You don't understand. Three thousand people flock to the Indian Room every day.

MARIUS. Three thousand people?

MADAME GABRIELLE. Three thousand people.

GEORGES. Yes. Volpini is kicking himself for having refused to take a percentage at the door.
But what you need to project these images is not a café, but a theatre.

MARIUS (*light dawning on him*). And boss, we've got a theatre!

53. 23 June 1984, 10.02 p.m., Paris

Offside

APRIL (*in the passenger seat of the car*)....So if the last defensive player is in front of the other team's attacker when he shoots, that's...

DECEMBER (*in the driver's seat in the car*). I don't know. Don't ask me. I've told you I'm not into football.

GERARD (*getting into the back seat of the car*). Offside is when a player is closer to the opponents' goal line than both the ball and the second-to-last player of the opposition, at the time his teammate passes him the ball. Easy!

DECEMBER. This is Gerard. He lent us his car.

APRIL. Gerard?

GERARD. I had planned on robbing the bank but DD forgot to tell me that there was no money in the safe during the building work.

APRIL. DD?

DECEMBER. Well, what are we going to do with this film?

GERARD. Film, what film?

LOUISE (*climbing into the back seat of the car*). We need an original kinetograph to project it.

GERARD. A what?

LOUISE. A kinetograph. Louise.

GERARD. Gerard.

APRIL. Louise is a real film buff.

LOUISE (*to* DECEMBER). I insisted on waiting for April, in case you weren't the right sort of guy. Delighted to meet you.

DECEMBER. Hi.

LOUISE (*to* APRIL). He seems nice?

APRIL. Well, shall we go?

DECEMBER. Where to?

GERARD. To find a kinetograph.

LOUISE. Bravo, Gerard.

DECEMBER. And where does one find a kinetograph?

LOUISE. Place du Trocadéro, at Chaillot, the film museum!

54. February 1896, Paris

Shop

GEORGES *has returned from England. He's grown a beard.*

GEORGES. Marius, we have to block up all the places where
the light gets in. Here, here and over there.

MARIUS. But, boss, this shop doesn't belong to us!

GEORGES. Ah? Go and see the surprise I've left you by the
door.

MADAME GABRIELLE. Mr Méliès. Did you have a good trip?

GEORGES. Terrible! The sea was rougher than ever.
What do you think of this shop?

MADAME GABRIELLE.…It's very dark. Quite small. Pretty
ugly.

GEORGES. Great. I've just bought it!
It'll be our laboratory.
We'll put the developer here and the fixer there.

MARIUS (*entering with the kinetograph*). What on earth's this
machine, boss?
It's like a giant coffee grinder!

GEORGES. May I present the kinetograph!

MARIUS. The what-o-what?

GEORGES. It's a Greek word: 'kineto' means motion; 'graph' means writing.

MARIUS. 'The motion of writing.'

GEORGES. The other way round.

MADAME GABRIELLE. 'The writing of motion.'

GEORGES. The way it works is very simple: you just turn the handle, at a regular speed. That'll be your job, Marius.

MARIUS. Why am I doing that?

GEORGES. We're taking pictures!
We're going to make moving pictures, like the Lumière brothers, which we'll then project in the theatre.

MADAME GABRIELLE. Pictures of what?

GEORGES. Everything. Anything.
A conjuring trick, learning how to ride a bicycle, a train arriving in a station… Life.

MADAME GABRIELLE. Sounds utterly stupid.

55. 1896, Paris

Performance

Evening performance. Screening of the first moving pictures. Enthusiastic response. GEORGES, MARIUS *and* MADAME GABRIELLE *watch their effect on the audience.*

MADAME GABRIELLE. Surprising.
I'll admit the audience seems to like it.

GEORGES. We can sell the moving pictures too. To theatre directors, funfairs. And we'll sell the machine with them.

MARIUS. Only these moving pictures?

GEORGES. We'll make lots of others. We'll film every day.

MADAME GABRIELLE. Every day?

GEORGES. Every day.

56. 1896, Paris

Programme

MADAME GABRIELLE *is jotting down the progamme to come in a notebook.*

MADAME GABRIELLE. So today we have the crowd in Place du Théâtre Français, the arrival of the train in Vincennes Station. Tomorrow we have the Bateaux Mouches, the Bois de Boulogne…

GEORGES. And a child playing with a ball.

MADAME GABRIELLE. Which doesn't tell much of a story. But if people like it…

GEORGES. What did you say?

MADAME GABRIELLE. I said if people like it…

GEORGES. No, the sentence before that.

MADAME GABRIELLE. That it doesn't tell much of a story. Actually, what I've noticed is the audience wants emotion, or humour, or thrills, in any case they want to be transported. They want to dream. Seeing babies and trains arriving is fun for a while. But then they'll go back to the theatre. But you're the boss. Don't take any notice of what I say…

GEORGES *is left alone onstage.*

GEORGES (*an idea suddenly comes to him*). Suzanne!

57. 1896, Paris

Invention

In the middle of the night, GEORGES *enters* SUZANNE*'s apartment.*

GEORGES. Suzanne, Suzanne, wake up!

SUZANNE. Georges?… what time is it?

GEORGES. Five o'clock.

SUZANNE (*lighting a lamp*). Five o'clock!

GEORGES. Suzanne, you know how we project the moving pictures we make at the theatre?

SUZANNE. How did you get in?

GEORGES. The door was open.
    The pictures are a big hit, Suzanne, but we're just copying. We're simply copying the Lumière brothers.

SUZANNE. Georges, it's five o'clock in the morning.

GEORGES. People will get tired of them. They'll end up wanting something new. They'll go back to the theatre.

SUZANNE (*turning out the light*). Well, let them go back. And you should go back to bed!

GEORGES. How are your performances going with Sarah Bernhardt?

SUZANNE. Brilliant. She's cut all my lines.

GEORGES. Suzanne, what if I offered you something better than the stage?

SUZANNE (*sighing*). Like going back to sleep?

GEORGES (*inventing the cinema*). Listen to me.
    The audience wants to be told a story.
    Nothing stopping me from using costumes, sets, special effects… like onstage.
    But with the kinetograph, there are no walls.

There's a framework, yes, but inside this framework,
everything is possible.
We can invent a new language, a new way of telling a story,
which'll be a mix of painting, music, magic... and will
remain forever imprinted on film.

SUZANNE. Georges, why are you telling me this at five
o'clock in the morning?

GEORGES. Because, Suzanne, I need an actress.

58. July 1896, Montreuil

The Vanishing Lady at the Théâtre Robert-Houdin

In Montreuil, GEORGES *has built a sort of little stage
complete with wooden sets.*
He is wearing his magician's costume. SUZANNE *is in a pretty
floral dress.*

MARIUS. You've built a set, boss?

GEORGES. I've just painted it. Put the machine here, Marius.

SUZANNE (*twirling around*). Do you like my dress?

GEORGES. Yes, yes, very much.
(*To* MARIUS.) Yesterday, when filming the Place de
L'Opéra, my camera broke down for a minute. Do you
remember?

MARIUS. Er... yes.

GEORGES. When we projected the film strip, it was like the
horse-drawn omnibus had been replaced by a hearse.

MARIUS. Yes, so?

GEORGES. I'm going to make Suzanne disappear.

SUZANNE. Again?

GEORGES....But this time, I'm going to make you disappear on film.

Marius, turn the handle.

MARIUS *does so*.

I make my entrance, bow to the audience, and call Suzanne. Stand over there.

I spread the newspaper on the ground, and place the chair on top of it.

Sit down, Suzanne.

Projected in the background, we begin to see Méliès' original film The Vanishing Lady.

SUZANNE. Like this?

GEORGES. Look straight at the kinetograph, as if it were the audience. I pick up a blanket, shake it out and then hide Suzanne underneath it.

SUZANNE. It's hot!

GEORGES. Then I take off the blanket, and... Marius stop!

MARIUS *stops turning the handle*.

The machine has stopped, Suzanne. You can go.

SUZANNE *slips away*.

Marius, start turning the handle again.

I shake the blanket and remove it! She has vanished!

Marius, what do you think about that?

MARIUS (*after a pause*)....Do you think there's really an audience for that, boss?

59. 23 June 1984, 10.22 p.m., Paris

Place du Trocadéro

In the car.

THE RADIO (*voice-over*). Ten minutes left to play.
France is still trailing, two goals to one.

GERARD. Come on!

THE RADIO (*voice-over*). It's looking more unlikely with
every passing second...

GERARD. Come on!

THE RADIO (*voice-over*). France will need a miracle to pull
this off ...

LOUISE (*switching off the radio, to* DECEMBER). April told
me that you were an orphan.

GERARD *switches the radio on again.*

THE RADIO (*voice-over*). A miracle, absolutely. That's the
right word.

LOUISE (*switching off the radio, to* DECEMBER). So you lost
both your parents?

DECEMBER. Yes, both.

LOUISE. Bit careless.

APRIL. Louise!

DECEMBER. Actually my mother gave birth to me
anonymously.

LOUISE. You've never tried to find her?

DECEMBER. Er...

LOUISE. Back in the day, they used to ask the mother to put
her name in a sealed envelope in case she died while giving
birth. Then that envelope could be opened by the child when
they reached the age of eighteen.

DECEMBER. Really?

GERARD. She never stops talking, does she?

APRIL. No.

GERARD. Shall we turn the match back on?

DECEMBER. No.

LOUISE. Anyways, that made loads of extra paperwork, so they gradually phased it out, and now all that data is entered into a computer system.

GERARD (*to* APRIL). How does she know all this?

APRIL. She's a ci…

LOUISE. I'm a proud civil servant. Just because I look the way I do and talk the way I talk, doesn't mean all the administrative paperwork of our Republic should be left to…

APRIL. Louise? Louise?

LOUISE. Sorry.

GERARD. Shall we turn the match back on?

DECEMBER *and* APRIL. No!

LOUISE. December, it's not exactly office hours, but it just so happens that at the moment I've employed an intern, Babacar, a young man from Sudan who's fled the political repression and poverty in his homeland, and as we now have a left-wing government, I think it's only right to give deserving cases…

APRIL. Louise…

LOUISE. Oh, sorry!

GERARD. Shall we turn the…?

DECEMBER *and* APRIL. NO!

LOUISE. In short, he's turned out to be brilliant on the computer, so I give him extra little tasks to do, which I make sure he's paid extra for, he's actually in the office today inputting data and I…

APRIL. Louise!

LOUISE.…and I'm going to call him! That's it, I've nothing else to say!

60. September 1896, Paris

Feature Film

GEORGES. My friends, we're going to make a feature film.

MARIUS. A what?

GEORGES. Not just twenty, not just forty, but sixty metres of film: over three minutes long!

The Devil's Castle. Suzanne will play the innocent young girl, and I will be the diabolical Mephistopheles.

MADAME GABRIELLE. Mr Méliès?
There are ten young women waiting to be seen by you!

SUZANNE. Ten young women?

MADAME GABRIELLE. For the position of 'colourist', they say.

GEORGES. Sign them all up!

SUZANNE. All of them?

GEORGES. The film will be in colour.

MARIUS. In colour? So each image will have to be coloured by hand?

GEORGES (*mischievously*). Precisely!

61. October 1896, Montreuil, Paris

Studio

In Montreuil, SUZANNE *is wearing the floral dress again.*

SUZANNE. I'm freezing!

GEORGES. What's the matter, Suzanne?

SUZANNE. I'm sorry but I'm cold. It is October.

MARIUS. Winter's coming, boss. We won't be able to film outside much longer.

GEORGES (*putting his coat around* SUZANNE*'s shoulders*). Go inside and get warm.

SUZANNE (*holding him back*). Mr Georges.

> SUZANNE *kisses* GEORGES, *tenderly at first, then passionately.*

MARIUS (*putting down the kinetograph*). There you go… (*Noticing the kiss.*) and there you go.

> SUZANNE *breaks away, and leaves the stage.*
> GEORGES *remains dumbfounded by the kiss.*

(*Changing the subject.*) Talking about inside, we'll need a room.

GEORGES. A room?

MARIUS. To shoot pictures in.

GEORGES. Ah, yes. It'll need a glass roof…

MARIUS (*light dawning*). A glass roof?… For the light, of course.

GEORGES. With a parquet floor, and a system of pullies for the backdrops. Like a theatre, but one reserved for shooting pictures.

MARIUS. Yes, but where are we going to find that?

GEORGES (*pointing to a corner of the garden*). Why not here?

MARIUS. Either I'm a complete idiot or I can only see a garden.

GEORGES. Imagine…

Chimney over there. Parquet floor here. The roof, up there, measuring seventeen metres by seven, a small stage five metres wide at one end, the machine at the other end.

MARIUS. Sounds great, boss! But who's going to build all that?

GEORGES *looks at* MARIUS *and smiles*.
MARIUS *rolls his eyes*.

62. 23 June 1984, 10.14 p.m., Place Du Trocadéro, Paris

Palais de Chaillot

THE TV (*voice-over*). Seven minutes left to play… seven minutes left to play and France is still down two goals to one. Six minutes now…

APRIL. The museum's upstairs.

Around them, the café terraces on the square are packed with people.

GERARD. Don't worry. We'll break a window, get into the theatre, climb up the wall and into the museum.

APRIL. Climb up the wall?!

GERARD. Piece of cake.

At the same time, LOUISE *is on the phone to Babacar:*

LOUISE. Hi, Babacar, it's Louise. Sorry to bother you… You're on a break watching the match?

THE TV (*voice-over*). And Giresse shoots! But it's blocked.

LOUISE. Well, okay, I won't tell anyone. But I have a little favour to ask you. Could you turn on the computer? Thanks.

THE TV (*voice-over*). Platini in the box who shoots but it's cleared away. Domergue is on the follow-up – it's a goal! A goal in the hundred and fourteenth minute! France are right back in this!

The entire square stands up at the same time. There's a huge cheer. Glasses are smashed, horns are honked, the noise is tremendous. GERARD breaks a window in the theatre.

DECEMBER. GOAL! GOAL!

THE TV (*voice-over*). France's dreams are still alive with a vital equaliser!

APRIL gives him a look.

DECEMBER. I was covering the noise of the –

APRIL. Just admit you're into football.

GERARD (*to* APRIL). Go ahead! I'll go and find your friend.

APRIL climbs through the broken window into the museum.

LOUISE (*screaming down the phone*). 'December', that's right, born on 9 December 1954, yes! Yes!

GERARD grabs LOUISE by the arm, pulling her off the phone.

GERARD. We've got to go! We've got to go!

He hangs up, banging the phone down.
LOUISE enters the museum, but GERARD's attention is on the match.

TWO–ALL!

DECEMBER takes him by the arm and pulls him towards the museum. He, too, is mesmerised by the match.

DECEMBER. GET IN!

APRIL comes to get him.

63. 16 February 1899, Montreuil, Paris

Star Films

MADAME GABRIELLE (*to the public at large*). Mr Méliès is very particular about the vocabulary used.
In the film studio, the machine is called a 'kinetograph', never a 'coffee grinder'. You are 'posers', not actors.
You will be paid twenty francs for each posing session.

MARIUS. Plus lunch.

MADAME GABRIELLE. For anyone who thinks that's not good enough, the door's over there.

MARIUS. Listen hard.
When Mr Méliès calls out 'Action', that means you start posing. When he calls out 'Cut!', the performance is over. Do you understand?

MADAME GABRIELLE.... They understand.

MARIUS (*to all at large*). Welcome to Star Films!

GEORGES. Marius!

MARIUS. Yes, boss?

GEORGES. Did you know that Félix Faure has just died?

MARIUS. Between the thighs of a young lady, yes, everyone knows that.

GEORGES. I want you to shoot the funeral. We'll send the film all over France.

MARIUS. I thought we didn't do politics.

GEORGES. This isn't politics, Marius, this is business! Madame Gabrielle?

MADAME GABRIELLE. Yes, Mr Méliès?

GEORGES. We're buying a stock of costumes from the Théâtre Français. Make an inventory of them, work out how much they're worth, then pay for them and send someone to fetch them.

MADAME GABRIELLE. Very good, Mr Méliès.

LUCIEN. Mr Méliès?

> *Enter* LUCIEN DE MAUROIS, *aged thirty.*
> *Very well dressed, a politician.*

GEORGES. I am the man himself.

LUCIEN. Lucien de Maurois, I work for the Republic.

GEORGES. We've already met, I believe?
(*Cordially.*) …Lucien! Suzanne's former suitor, with the great prospects! How are you?

LUCIEN (*coldly*). I have come to ask you to work for the French government.

GEORGES. The French government, no less. Madame Gabrielle!

MADAME GABRIELLE. Mr Méliès?

GEORGES. What's our turnover this year?

MADAME GABRIELLE. Ninety thousand gold francs.

GEORGES. I'm not a civil servant, Lucien. I enjoy my independence too much to sell to the government.

LUCIEN. I would strongly advise you to work for us.

GEORGES. So we've already jumped from a proposition to advice?
What next? Threats?
I bid you good day, Mr de Maurois.

64. 1899

Pathé Films

LUCIEN. Mr Pathé?

CHARLES. Charles, call me Charles.

LUCIEN. Did you know that Georges Méliès has decided to produce a series of films on Captain Dreyfus?

CHARLES. A series? What an excellent idea. That boy is diabolically inventive.

LUCIEN. You could make a copy?

CHARLES. I fear I misheard you.

LUCIEN (*after a pause*). You see, when it comes to cinematographic copyright, there's a legal void at the moment. Méliès is a brilliant inventor, but you are a far shrewder entrepreneur. You are currently at liberty to reproduce all his moving pictures identically and then you could distribute them far wider than he would ever be able to.

CHARLES. Leave this office, sir.

LUCIEN. Mr Pathé…

CHARLES. Leave!
Never in my life, do you hear, would I, Charles Pathé, stoop to such a vile practice!

LUCIEN *leaves*.
CHARLES, *after a while, goes to the door.*

Mademoiselle Josiane.

MADEMOISELLE JOSIANE. Yes, Monsieur Pathé?

CHARLES. Send somebody discreet to purchase all the moving pictures made by Georges Méliès. Including his most recent ones. And bring them to me.

MADEMOISELLE JOSIANE. Very well, Monsieur Pathé!

65. 1902, Montreuil, Paris

Westminster in Montreuil

WILLIAM. Georges!

> WILLIAM *and* GEORGES *greet each other with a hug.*

GEORGES. Willy, how are you?

WILLIAM. Never been better, old chap. Even though it's ruddy cold here, at least it's not raining.

GEORGES. What brings you to France?

WILLIAM. I've got a marvellous idea for you, Georges. You know our dear Queen Victoria died last year?

GEORGES. Yes.

WILLIAM. Well the new king, Edward VII, will be crowned in Westminster Abbey in a few weeks.

GEORGES. Do you want me to film it?

WILLIAM. No.

GEORGES. No?

WILLIAM. No. The problem is that you won't be allowed into the Abbey, old boy.

GEORGES. Ah.

WILLIAM. However, you could shoot the procession arriving in Westminster.

GEORGES. Yes, but I'd want the interior too?

WILLIAM (*smiling*).…What if you reconstructed it in Montreuil?

GEORGES. In Montreuil?

WILLIAM. In Montreuil. With posers, costumes, a set…

GEORGES (*with stars in his eyes*).…We'd need a massive set.

WILLIAM. Huge.

> *The two men exchange looks.*

GEORGES. We could use the hangar adjoining the studio.

WILLIAM. You like the idea! Jolly good!

GEORGES. I'd need photos of all the members of the royal family.

WILLIAM. You'll have them! All of them!
I know the master of ceremony. He'll give me all the details.

GEORGES. The result would have to be as realistic as the original.

WILLIAM. More realistic!

GEORGES (*calling out*). Madame Gabrielle, Marius, everyone, come here!

66. 1902, Paris

Coronation

LUCIEN. Mr Méliès?

GEORGES. Luicen! How's the Republic getting along?

LUCIEN. And you, how are you?

GEORGES. Madame Gabrielle, the turnover?

MADAME GABRIELLE. Three hundred and fifty thousand gold francs, Mr Méliès.

LUCIEN (*after a pause*). We saw the Coronation.

GEORGES. Mine or the other one?

LUCIEN. Your result was strikingly real.
Did you know that the ceremony was postponed for a few weeks, on the other side of the Channel?

GEORGES (*smiling*). Yes, I was informed.

LUCIEN. Your fiction preceded reality.
  The King of England was crowned in French cinemas even
  before he became King in London. Work for us, Georges.

GEORGES. What would you want me to do?

LUCIEN. We would like you to improve certain images of
  current events. Finesse the truth.

GEORGES. You mean to make fake pictures?

LUCIEN. You'd have carte blanche.

  GEORGES *seems to hesitate for a moment*.

GEORGES. Power is an illusion, Lucien.
  For every madman who believes he can crush people
  underfoot, there's always a bigger foot, belonging to another
  madman, ready to trample upon him.

  I myself am the captain of a majestic vessel, a vessel that
  may hold Humanity in its entirety, transcending age, origin
  and beliefs, a vessel whose sole purpose is the voyage itself.
  And do you know what my next destination will be, Mr de
  Maurois?

LUCIEN. Africa? Asia?

GEORGES. The Moon, Mr Undersecretary. Nothing less than
  the Moon.

67. 23 June 1984, 10.17 p.m., Paris

The World is a Ship

GERARD. Pay attention now: I'm going to turn the handle.

  GERARD *manages to get Méliès' old machine working.
  Fascinated, they watch his* A Trip to the Moon.

THE WATCHMAKER. The world is a vast ship,
  which carries three kinds of passengers:

those who want to know,
those who already know,
and those who dream.

LOUISE. December, I've discovered who your parents were.

DECEMBER. Pardon?

LOUISE. Babacar found them.
Your mother is deceased, but your father is still alive.
We have several copies of his employment certificates.
He's been working in the same place for twenty-five years.

DECEMBER. In France?

LOUISE. In Paris.

DECEMBER. In Paris?

LOUISE. Yes. In a tiny shop in the Place Vendôme.

DECEMBER. What does he do?

LOUISE. He's a craftsman, a watchmaker.

A Trip to the Moon *suddenly stops, replaced by a blank*
screen, then covered in flames.
The film and the camera catch fire.

APRIL. It's on fire. It's on fire!

GERARD. Ah, shit, the camera! The film!

LOUISE. Fire! Fire!

GERARD *takes off his jacket, throws it over the kinetograph*
and puts out the flames.
The fire is out, silence returns to the theatre.
They all seem stunned for a moment.

TRANSISTOR RADIO (*commentary heard faintly offstage*).
Winning is not going to be easy; in any case it looks like
we're heading for a penalty shoot-out...

The little transistor is hanging from the waist of a NIGHT
WATCHMAN.
In his left hand, he is carrying a torch. In his right, a cosh.

THE NIGHT WATCHMAN. Forced entry into the museum,
a broken window, a kicked-in door, and if that wasn't enough
you set an original kinetograph on fire.

On the night of the match. Why couldn't you have stayed at
home?

TRANSISTOR RADIO (*voice-over*). Only two minutes left on
the clock. Fernandez goes long to Tigana, who carries the
ball down the wing.

THE NIGHT WATCHMAN (*turning up the volume*).
Goddamn!

GERARD. Yes! Go for it, Tigana!

THE NIGHT WATCHMAN (*turning up the volume even
louder*). Shh!

TRANSISTOR RADIO (*voice-over*)….Tigana tries a pass, it's
blocked, comes straight back to him, he's driving into the
box, looks for an option, finds Platini –

GERARD. Come on!

TRANSISTOR RADIO (*voice-over*). Platini collects the ball,
he shoots… he scores!

GERARD. Goal! Goal!

TRANSISTOR RADIO (*voice-over*). Unbelievable!! Michel
Platini has scored in the hundred and nineteenth minute!

GERARD. Three–two?

THE NIGHT WATCHMAN. Three–two!

GERARD. Are we in the final?

THE NIGHT WATCHMAN. WE'RE IN THE FINAL!

GERARD *headbutts* THE NIGHT WATCHMAN, *who falls
to the ground*.

GERARD. And now, I suggest we run for it.

68. 23 June 1984, 10.19 p.m., Place Du Trocadéro, Paris

Final

There's almost a riot in the square.
One minute left to play and France will qualify for the final.

APRIL. The car! Where's the car?

DECEMBER. Over there, it's over there.

  GERARD *stops outside a café.*

LOUISE. Are you coming, Gerard?

GERARD (*hypnotised by the match*). I'm coming! There's only
  one minute to go!

LOUISE. Men and football? Like where did this infantile
  infatuation actually…

GERARD. Just shut up for once and watch!

  DECEMBER *and* APRIL *find themselves alone.*

DECEMBER. Where the hell is it?

APRIL. What?

DECEMBER. The car!

  The final whistle blows.

THE TV (*voice-over*). And it's the end of the match! France is
  in the final!

  Paris explodes with joy. Everyone starts hugging each other.
  APRIL *and* DECEMBER *exchange looks.*

DECEMBER. We're in the final.

APRIL. We're in the final! I suppose football can be exciting.

DECEMBER. Yes… Can I kiss you?

APRIL. Yes.

DECEMBER. Yes?

  APRIL *moves towards him, then suddenly draws back.*

APRIL. No, December. I'm engaged.

DECEMBER. Yes, yes. Of course, sorry.

APRIL. But it's complicated. It's not going very well. Just kiss me.

DECEMBER. Okay.

APRIL (*draws back again*). No, December. I'm pregnant.

DECEMBER. Yes, yes, of course, sorry.

APRIL. I'm pregnant by you.

DECEMBER.... What?

APRIL. You see, I've always wanted a child.

DECEMBER. But April, I haven't even kissed you yet.

APRIL. Listen, I got together with a guy who's nice but it always felt like something was missing. It's not been working. I thought a child would help...

DECEMBER. Ah.

APRIL. I know, know. But he can't have kids...

DECEMBER. Er...

APRIL. We tried everything but it didn't work, so finally I went to this clinic, where men donate and that's where it did work... But it hasn't fixed anything – if anything it's made us drift further apart.

DECEMBER. April?

APRIL.... and the only thing I knew about the biological father was that he'd left a book behind at the clinic, an old book about magic.

DECEMBER. Oh, shit.

APRIL. And I didn't think any more about it until the day I found that inscription on the bank vault. And then I understood. I understood that it was fate.

DECEMBER (*beginning to understand*). Oh, shit...

APRIL. So I bribed the secretary at the clinic into giving me the father's name. And that's you.

DECEMBER. Oh, shit! I was broke... It was so long ago. At that time I thought I never wanted to be a father... that was all supposed to be anonymous.

APRIL. I employed a private detective to find you and I deliberately dropped my bag in front of you. All I wanted to do was return your book, but you phoned me. December, you phoned me back!

DECEMBER. You're completely out of your mind!

THE CAFÉ OWNER. So, you lovebirds, we're in the final!

DECEMBER. What?

THE CAFÉ OWNER. By the way, if you're looking for your car, it's over there.

DECEMBER. How do you know that?

THE CAFÉ OWNER (*on the way out*). I know a lot of things! I've had so many lives...

DECEMBER (*to* APRIL). Drunk.

APRIL (*following him*). December, listen, I'm in love with you. In a way that I've never felt before. And now as if by magic. Chance. Fate. A reality neither of us dared to dream. Me, you, our child!

DECEMBER. But, I'd given up on all that. April...

APRIL. December, April, April, December!

DECEMBER. But dammit, April, fate doesn't exist!

APRIL. One thousand! Plus forty!

DECEMBER. April.

APRIL. Plus a thousand! Plus thirty!

DECEMBER. April.

APRIL. Plus a thousand!

> DECEMBER *finally kisses her.*
> *The music crescendos. A long kiss, then:*

DECEMBER. April, we come from different worlds. How could it work?

APRIL. It'll work.

DECEMBER. Why?

APRIL. Because I'm carrying our son.

DECEMBER.... A son? How do you know that it's a son?

APRIL. I'm sure of it. Women feel these things, December. It's a boy, our boy.

69. 28 June 2000, Montreuil, Paris

Epilogue

The doorbell rings. Fifteen years later.

DECEMBER. Jeanne! JEANNE!
Answer the door!

> DECEMBER *calls out to his fifteen-year-old daughter,*
> JEANNE.
> *He's wearing a dark suit.*

JEANNE. Daaaad, I'm in the middle of playing...

She's playing video games.

DECEMBER. ANSWER THE DOOR!

JEANNE. Ask Mum!

DECEMBER. She's already waiting in the car. Go and open the door, it'll be Grandad!

JEANNE. You're really bloody annoying, dammit!

She presses 'pause' and goes to answer the door.

DECEMBER (*stopping her on the way*). Wait, wait a minute,
sweetheart!
(*Opening his arms wide.*) How do I look?

JEANNE. Old.

DECEMBER. Right.

Also not the right time, but… your mother and I were
wondering, any decisions about what you want to do
next year?

JEANNE (*sighing*). ARGH… really? Do you want me to open
the door or not?

DECEMBER. Answer me first.

JEANNE (*mumbling*). Makevideogames…

DECEMBER. Pardon?

JEANNE. I want to make video games.

DECEMBER *sighs*.

In fact… I've thought of something.

DECEMBER *listens, hopefully*.

Promise you won't be sarcastic?

DECEMBER. Go on.

JEANNE (*explaining all in a rush*). Wouldn't it be great if you
could play without joysticks?

DECEMBER. Jeanne…

JEANNE.…if you could play with your hands. Your hands
would be the joysticks.
And with cameras. Maybe with like three cameras placed
around the TV, you could…

DECEMBER. Jeanne.

JEANNE. Yes?

DECEMBER. And besides video games?

JEANNE....I hate you.

GRANDFATHER *enters. Obviously it's* THE
WATCHMAKER.

GRANDFATHER. Hello, sweetheart, how's life?

JEANNE (*going back to her game*). Super. Looking forward to
watching football with you, but before it starts I just need to
finish this game.

GRANDFATHER (*to* DECEMBER). Go on then. And you, how
are you?

DECEMBER. Super. How did you get in?

GRANDFATHER. By magic... April let me in.
Not tempted to watch the match? France against Portugal?

DECEMBER. No. We're eating out. It's a tradition.

GRANDFATHER. The Euro 2000 semi-final?
Zidane, Desailly, Deschamps...

DECEMBER. I know, I know, don't rub it in. Anyway, we
won't repeat the win of 1984, that was magic.

GRANDFATHER. You never know

DECEMBER (*kissing him goodbye*). Thanks, Dad.

GRANDFATHER . My pleasure.

DECEMBER (*loudly*). Bye, sweetheart!

She doesn't answer.

(*To his father.*) She wants to make video games.

APRIL (*entering*). What are you doing? Are we going? Or you
could stay and watch the match?

DECEMBER (*on the way out*). Why would I do that? I'm
coming! I'm coming!

APRIL. Thank you, Michel. Bye, Jeanne.

She doesn't answer.

Good luck.

GRANDFATHER. Have a nice evening.

Exit DECEMBER *and* APRIL.
JEANNE *is sitting in front of her video game.*
GRANDFATHER *watches her for a moment.*

Your turn will come, young Jeanne.
You'll do great things.

JEANNE. What did you say?

GRANDFATHER. Nothing, nothing.
Keep on playing.

The lights are dimmed. JEANNE *gradually disappears.*

70.

A Red Scarf

THE WATCHMAKER. The hands of time turn inexorably,
but the hand of man has limitless power.
Clenched, it can start a rebellion, federate or strike.
Open, it can caress, carry or create.

One can also pull a red scarf from it. (*He pulls out a red scarf.*)

This scarf comes from another world, a fantastic universe
In which, for the space of a moment, the audience can take refuge,
While keeping their eyes wide open.
The scarf then goes back inside the hand.
The magician blows on it, and it disappears.

Blackout.

www.nickhernbooks.co.uk

facebook.com/nickhernbooks

twitter.com/nickhernbooks